# Sermon on the Mount

# Sermon on the Mount

**CLARENCE JORDAN**

A Koinonia Publication
JUDSON PRESS, Valley Forge

SERMON ON THE MOUNT

Copyright © 1952
Judson Press
Valley Forge, Pa. 19481

Koinonia Edition 1970
Second Printing, 1971

International Standard Book No. 0-8170-0501-3

Printed in the U.S.A.

# Contents

1. Before the Sermon Begins    9

2. Stairway to Spiritual Life, Part 1    17

3. Stairway to Spiritual Life, Part 2    27

4. The Effect of the Christian Community
   on the World    36

5. Things New and Old, Part 1    45

6. Things New and Old, Part 2    54

7. Things New and Old, Part 3    63

8. Testing Our Motives, Part 1    72

9. Testing Our Motives, Part 2    81

10. The Measure of a Treasure    90

11. Danger of Self-Righteous Judging    99

12. Power Through Faith and Discipline    108

13. Clear Call to Christian Action    117

# 1   Before the Sermon Begins

"And seeing the multitudes, he went up into the mountain: and when he had sat down, his disciples came unto him: and he opened his mouth and taught them . . ." (Matthew 5:1-2).
*Read Matthew 4:17—5:2.*

They were young, and life pressed in on their hearts like steam in an unpopped kernel of popcorn just before it explodes. They wanted action, adventure, achievement, happiness. To be sure, they lived nearly two thousand years ago, but that does not alter the fact that they desired to make their lives count significantly. Like all Jewish young people of that day, they grew up with a keen sense of responsibility toward God and toward their nation. They believed that they were prepared to pay whatever price they would be called upon to make to serve both God and country.

But there were problems — big problems. In their personal lives these twelve men had not begun to face their inner fears. Despite their loud laughter and surface gaiety, inwardly they were as uncertain as swamp muck — and they knew it. Just to look at them, you'd think they had never had a care in the world and had never given much real thought to the big issues of life. That's because with the physical eye you cannot see anxiety and greed and selfishness and lust and hate. But you sense these things and know that they are real. Yes, these men had thought a lot about God and prayer and faith and sincerity and loyalty, yet they were far from any clear understanding of these things.

There was also another set of problems caused by the world situation. Their country was occupied by the tyrannical military government of Rome, so there was the ever-present question of the right attitude toward these enemies. Race prejudice was so prevalent that a fellow hardly knew who his neighbor was. The staggering taxes, already about a third of one's paycheck, kept alive the problem of what one would eat or drink or wear. The middle class of people had almost disappeared; there were only the very rich and the very poor. Slavery was rampant. It was a dark hour indeed.

All kinds of answers were being proposed. Some people said, "It's no use. Quit trying. The thing to do is to go ahead and enjoy yourself while you can. Eat, drink, and have a good time; you'll be dying soon." Others said, "Grit your teeth and bear it. Show people how strong you are by never complaining." A bunch of fanatics called Zealots said, "Don't mope about the inner life. We must win our national freedom. Our only hope is a mighty army." The Sadducees felt about the same way, except they were not as outspoken. They were great at compromising, for it always seemed to work out to their personal advantage. With equal ease they could do business with Rome or their countrymen, with good or with evil. They answered by never really facing life. "If you can't dodge an issue," they said in essence, "make the best possible bargain in your favor."

The Pharisees saw things differently. They felt that if you lived a clean, pure life (as defined by the rabbis) and trusted God, he would do all the rest. Life would work only one way, and that was in slavish obedience to God, for he was a strict, severe taskmaster who allowed no deviation from the straight line of the law. In return for this scrupulous obedience, God would prosper men and charge his angels to keep watch over them. The Pharisees thought they had a much nicer arrangement than the Sadducees. The Sadducees bargained with Rome; the Pharisees bargained with God.

In the midst of this wild clamor, the quiet One climbed Judea's hills and walked the plains of Galilee. He knew the people — their hopes and fears, their longings and frustrations, their confusion and hunger; he knew they were like sheep without a shepherd. And it was no secret that he had tremendous power over them. He had authority. They knew it, and he knew it.

He loved them and wanted to be their spiritual king. What would he offer them? Would they accept him?

With all the man-made panaceas and propositions seething in his head, he went into the wilderness. So great was his concern that for days he gave no thought to food. In his acute hunger, he was beset with the temptation to turn the stones around him on the hillside into bread. If he were really God's Son, surely this request would not be denied him, for even a human father would not give his son a stone if he asked for bread. If he were not God's Son, of course he had no right to claim the throne and declare the establishment of the kingdom of God on earth. His whole ministry and message seemed to hinge on one question: "Are you the Son of God or not?"

On the surface, this bread-making seemed like a fair

proposition. And it would be a clear-cut answer to the question of Sonship. Yet, with his penetrating insight, Jesus saw that a bread-and-butter arrangement was no basis for Sonship. That was the relationship between master and slave. Bread alone would meet neither his needs nor those of kingdom citizens. To be sure, there must be provision in his kingdom for physical needs, but the Father-Son relationship would be infinitely more than that.

Then came the temptation to side with the Zealots and to establish a political world order built on force and violence. He repudiated this with great finality. He said in effect, "A true son will do his father's will. It is not the Father's purpose to establish a kingdom in which men fight." (See John 18:36.) "Therefore, to participate would be to deny my Sonship."

But what would he say to the Pharisees? What was wrong with their plan of climbing to the very pinnacle of all that the temple stood for — a severe, religious life of ritual, rules, and external ethics — and then casting one's self entirely upon the mercy of the Lord? "But," he might have asked, "why bargain with God? Why put him to the test? Why experiment with him?" A true son would commit himself unreservedly to his father, whether or not it "paid off" or was "practical." Was he willing to make a total commitment with no ifs and buts, and then take the consequences? Yes! And in order to establish his kingdom on earth, he must ask his subjects to make the same commitment! Their loyalty must be for better or for worse, until death.

Having completely rejected, then, the way of materialism and force, and having utterly abandoned himself, with no strings attached, to the Father, "From that time Jesus began to preach and to say, Repent ye; for the kingdom of heaven is at hand" (Matthew 4:17; see also Matthew 3:2).

For unbelievers, Jesus had but one word: "RE-PENT." It's a tremendous word. We must examine it. The Greek word from which it is translated means "to change one's mind for the better, heartily to amend with abhorrence of one's past sins" (*Thayer's Lexicon*). So when he called on men to repent, he really demanded that they change their way of thinking, abandon their false concepts, forsake their wrong methods, and enter upon a new way of life. Imagine what this meant to the Pharisees whose "good behavior" and whose "trust in the Lord" assured them of the divine favor. Weren't they already saved, and just about the best people God had on earth? Yet Jesus felt that of all people, these had the greatest need of changing their ways. He also told the wealthy, aristocratic, unscrupulous Sadducees to change their way of living. He called on the super-patriotic, military-minded Zealots to change their attitudes. He faced all these men, as he does their spiritual descendants today, with that one terrific word: *repent!*

No one has a right, however, to call on men to change their ways *unless he has a more excellent way to offer.* Forsaking the wrong way is only half of repentance; accepting the right way is the other half. The call to repentance, then, must always be accompanied by the glorious announcement, "for the kingdom of God is here!" Jesus proclaimed it as "the good news." For him, it was the way, the only way, for men to live. Only when men had accepted the kingdom could it be said that they had truly repented. To enter it was to be saved, to find eternal life. (See Luke 18:18, 24, 26 where finding eternal life, entering the kingdom, and being saved seem to refer to the same thing.)

It is with this kingdom that the Sermon on the Mount concerns itself. We shall be better prepared to understand this great discourse of the Master's if, before entering upon a study of it, we keep constantly before us certain things about the kingdom.

First, its foundation is the revelation that God is a Father, that Jesus Christ is his Son and the rightful Lord of the faithful, and that the Holy Spirit is the guide of all citizens of the kingdom. Believers, by identification with the Son, become sons of the Father. The result is a brotherhood, or family, of those who so believe.

Second, in this new relationship men can have no conflicting loyalties. The kingdom takes precedence over everything else —occupation (Matthew 4:20), family ties (Matthew 4:22; Luke 14:26), and possessions (Luke 14:33). One should be fully warned of this before going in quest of the kingdom. It should be made clear, however, that while one might be called upon at any time to give up these lesser pearls, he will be the possessor of a pearl of infinitely greater value. To accept the kingdom means to put first things first.

Third, the kingdom is not a department of life set off to itself, but like blood in the body, it extends to *every* area of man's life. It makes adequate provision for *all* human need, whether it be spiritual ("They brought to him the demon-possessed"), mental (". . . and the lunatics"), or physical (". . . and the paralytics") and he healed them all (Matthew 4:24). That his concept of the kingdom included the whole man is also seen in his threefold ministry of preaching (spiritual), teaching (mental), and healing (physical). To him the kingdom of God was far more than a religious interest; it was *the way of life*.

Fourth, the doors of the kingdom are open to all men without respect to race, class, caste, color, nationality, education, or wealth. The children of God are under divine compulsion to accept as a brother *any* man who repents and believes. Inside the kingdom there are no partitions. He who would erect them thereby declares himself to be on the outside.

Now, just a few words about the Sermon itself. It is recorded by Matthew in chapters 5–7, and by Luke, in a somewhat different and abbreviated form, in chapter 6:17-49. While both accounts will be considered, our study will center upon Matthew's presentation.

Some people feel that the Sermon really wasn't a sermon, but a number of Jesus' sayings which the early church collected and put together. This may be true; we just don't know. The main thing, however, is that Jesus said them, whether in one discourse or many. They are genuine, and being his, they are authoritative. It is my belief that instead of being a collection of sayings, the Sermon is a *condensation* of a much longer discourse. We do know that multitudes continued with him for as long as three days at a time (Matthew 15:32), and while he did much healing then, he no doubt also used the opportunity to teach and pray at great length. Matthew 15:29 says: ". . . And he went up into the mountain, and sat there." It was the custom to sit while preaching or teaching. Compare that verse with Matthew 5:1, "He went up into the mountain: and when he had sat down. . . ." So it could be possible that the Sermon is a condensation of what he spoke about during the three days prior to the feeding of the four thousand.

Another thing: So lofty are the ethical precepts of the Sermon that many people have deified it and relegated the preacher to the role of a lesser prophet. "It doesn't matter what you believe about Jesus," these people say. "The Sermon on the Mount is my creed!" Still others would try to cling to Jesus and throw out the Sermon. But the two must never be separated. It is as impossible to dissociate a man from his message as a tree from its sap. They belong together. You can't fully understand one apart from the other.

So it would be unfair to ask you to accept the Sermon without accepting Jesus, and vice versa. If it is your intention to leave Jesus out of your life, it would be well not to make this study, for apart from him, his Sermon is senseless idealism — an impossible, frustrating, ethic. It might even make you bitter and cynical.

If you have already accepted him but have not realized and committed yourself to the tremendous personal and social teachings of the Sermon, this study might save you from an unreal, emotional mysticism.

Finally, lest you should run in vain, burn upon your heart the words with which the Lord closed the discourse: "He that heareth these words of mine, and *doeth* them, is like a *wise* man. . . ." "He that heareth and doeth not, is like a fool. . . ." Thus Jesus put *action* into the very core of the Christian life. Real learning comes through doing. In this, the Holy Spirit will be your guide.

# 2 Stairway to Spiritual Life Part 1

"Blessed are the poor in spirit: for theirs is the kingdom of heaven.
"Blessed are they that mourn: for they shall be comforted.
"Blessed are the meek: for they shall inherit the earth"
　　(Matthew 5:3-5).

Crowds always moved Jesus. Sometimes the sight of them moved him to great compassion; at other times their disbelief aroused his pity; their selfishness caused him to wonder if they were following him only for the loaves and fishes; the prevalence of sickness and disease among them gnawed at his heart; and their lostness and confusion filled him with a desire to show them the true way to life.

"And seeing the multitudes, he went up into the mountain." The sight of common, ordinary folk such as one might see on any busy street, or at a football game, or in a bus station, inspired the greatest teaching ever given to humanity. But while they were ordinary people, it wasn't an ordinary crowd. For one thing, they were all aware that their world was crashing down upon them, that their civilization was sick unto death, that they had about reached the end of their rope. For another thing, they were a crowd that had been faced with the summons to repent. They were about ready to admit that the old way had failed, and with but little persuasion they would gladly forsake it, but they needed to know more about this new way. Even though it made good sense, it did not follow accepted patterns. And to change one's mind on such basic issues called for plenty of thought and careful investigation. They just weren't prepared yet to repent fully; that is, to forsake their wrong ways and accept the Right Way, or the kingdom.

One of the purposes of the Sermon, then, was to present the good news of the kingdom so clearly and so convincingly that the people would repent and make *the great decision*. Viewed in this light, it is the most evangelistic Sermon ever preached. To evangelize means to preach the good news of Christ and his kingdom so as to convict men of the error of their former ways and to convince them of the rightness of the new way, the result being a commitment of life to life for life. Surely the Sermon on the Mount qualifies for that. The people are faced here not with the good news *about* Christ but with Christ himself. The gospel of the kingdom is proclaimed not by a deputy but by the king himself. The inadequacy of the old righteousness is vividly contrasted with the superlative quality of the new: "Ye have heard that it was said by them of old times . . . but I say unto you . . . Except your righteousness *exceed* the righteousness of the scribes and Pharisees. . . ." The Sermon is then brought to a dramatic conclusion with a powerful exhortation to definite action and commitment.

The kingdom of God on earth is Jesus' specific proposal to mankind. While the Sermon on the Mount is not a complete statement of the proposal (it takes all four Gospels for that), it does contain many of the major points. So it is quite natural at the very beginning for Jesus to deal with the question of how to enter the kingdom, or how to become a citizen of it.

The first seven Beatitudes do just that. They are the steps into the kingdom, the stairway to spiritual life. They are not disconnected, isolated "sayings," but a definite whole with each step, or Beatitude, arranged progressively and in order. The "poor in spirit" ascend the steps and become "sons of God." This Father-son relationship places men in the beloved community, the society of sinners saved by grace, the family of the Father, the kingdom of God. We see, then, that these are not blessings pronounced upon different kinds of people — the meek, the merciful, the pure in heart, and so on. Rather, they are stages in the experience of only one class of people — those who are entering the kingdom and who at each stage are blessed. The kingdom, of course, is *the* blessing, and each step into it partakes of its blessedness. This blessedness comes with the taking of the step, and is not postponed as a future reward. Jesus said, "Blessed *are.* ..."

But if these Beatitudes are stairsteps into the kingdom, each one rising above the other, where does the new birth come in, which John's Gospel emphatically declares is essential to entering the kingdom? (John 3:3 — "Jesus answered and said unto him, Verily, verily, I say unto thee, Except one be born anew, he cannot see the kingdom of God.") Does Jesus in the Gospel of Matthew give one requirement for entering the kingdom and Jesus in the Gospel of John give another?

No, they're both the same. Though Matthew does not use the term "the new birth," the Beatitudes seem to be a detailed explanation of it. And while John doesn't give the Beatitudes, the figure of birth is apparently used to illustrate them. Whether we call the process Beatitudes or birth, the result is the same: "sons of God." Both accounts agree that sonship is a basic requirement for membership in the Father's family.

The first step in becoming a son, or being begotten from above, or in entering the kingdom, or being saved, or finding eternal life — whatever term you wish to use — is stated by Jesus as:

*"The poor in spirit are partakers of the divine blessing, for theirs is the kingdom of heaven."*\*

What does Jesus mean by "poor in spirit"? In Luke's account it is simply "you poor." What kind of poverty is he talking about? If you have a lot of money, you'll probably say spiritual poverty. If you have little or no money, you'll probably say physical poverty. The rich will thank God for Matthew; the poor will thank God for Luke. Both will say, "He blessed *me!*" Well, then, who really did get the blessing?

Chances are, neither one. For it is exactly this attitude of self-praise and self-justification and self-satisfaction that robs men of a sense of great need for the kingdom and its blessings. When one says, "I don't need to be poor in things; I'm poor in spirit," and another says, "I don't need to be poor in spirit; I'm poor in things," both are justifying themselves as they are, and are saying in unison, "I don't need." With that cry on his lips, no man can repent.

\*Translation by the author. All future New Testament quotations within the chapters, unless otherwise stated, will also be the author's translation.

The story of the Pharisee and the publican (Luke 18:10-14) illustrates this. It doesn't say that the Pharisee was rich. It's quite probable that he was rather poor, since he thanked God, sincerely we presume, that he was not an extortioner like other men. At that time extortion was about the only respectable means of amassing a fortune, so "extortioner" and "rich man" were practically synonymous. It doesn't say either that the publican was poor. If he was a sample publican, he was rich, for publicans were notorious "extortioners." Anyway, the point is that regardless of outward circumstances, the Pharisee expressed an inner need for nothing — and that's what he got. The publican, admitting his sin, expressed a deep need for God's mercy — and that's what he got. *Each received what he felt he needed.*

That this element of need is the first essential to kingdom citizenship is seen in the severe warning to the church at Laodicea. "I know your ways . . . I am about to eject you, because you say, 'I am rich and prosperous and I don't have need of a thing.' And you don't know that you are a miserable wretch, a blind, naked beggar! Take my advice and get some real gold from me so that you might be truly rich, and clean clothes so that your shameful nakedness might be covered, and some eye-medicine so you might see" (Revelation 3:15, 17-18). This church had plenty of money, but it wasn't "poor in spirit." Its material wealth robbed it of a sense of spiritual need. Probably because money has this power to rob, Jesus said it was extremely difficult for a rich man to enter the kingdom, and that is why he looked at his *disciples* and said, "Blessed are *ye* poor." Not having money to deceive them, the poor should find it easier to recognize their need. But it is neither wealth nor poverty that keeps men out of the kingdom — *it is pride.*

So the poor in spirit are not the proud in spirit. They know that in themselves — in all mankind — there are few, if any, spiritual resources. They must have help from above. They desperately need the kingdom of heaven. And feeling their great need for the kingdom, *they get it.* "For theirs is the kingdom of heaven." Nobody else ever gets it, for the simple reason that they don't want it. God does not force his kingdom upon anybody but gladly gives it to all who know they're losers without him and humbly seek his help.

With one's pride gone, with one's trust in self and intellect and possessions gone, one is now ready to take the second step into the kingdom. Jesus says, "The mourners are partakers of the divine blessing, for they are the ones who shall be strengthened." Surely he doesn't mean it just like that, we say to ourselves. Why does he want people to mourn? Religion is too sad-eyed already. Life should be young and gay. Besides, how are you going to get into the kingdom by crying about it? Bawling about a thing never did any good. You must *do* something. And around and around certain well-intentioned people go today trying to get you to *do* something to be saved.

But strange as it seems, this Beatitude says that you must mourn. A mourner is not necessarily one who weeps. He is one who expresses a deep concern. If the one about whom he is concerned dies, he might express his grief by crying; he might also do it by praying, or in some other way. Tears aren't essential to mourning, *but deep concern is.*

With this in mind, let's try to see what Jesus means. He has already said that before you can get into the kingdom, you must recognize your own spiritual poverty and be conscious of your need of the kingdom. That's very, very important, but it's not enough. There must be a concern about this bankrupt condition so deep that it will find some expression. We must be *really grieved* that things are as they are. Those people are not real mourners who say, "Sure, the world's in a mess, and I guess maybe I'm a bit guilty like everybody else, but what can I do about it?" What they're really saying is that they are not concerned enough about themselves or the world to *look* for anything to do. No great burden hangs on their hearts. They aren't grieved. They don't mourn.

The kingdom citizen is different. There is no joy for him in idly contemplating his miserable failures. He's sick, and he knows it, but he wants to get well. His deep concern leads him to definite action; he goes to the doctor.

So the mourners are really those who are *concerned to the point of action*. This explains why "they shall be comforted," or better, "strengthened," or "encouraged." When a man limits his concern to talk and study and is an active member of a committee to draw up some resolutions, he is not much of a force to be reckoned with. He is easily and soon discouraged. But you'd better watch out when a fellow gets that certain gleam in his eye and a certain set to his jaw. He's getting ready to "mourn." And he'll be awfully hard to stop, because he will be receiving tremendous strength and power and encouragement from seeing his dreams become deeds. He probably won't be comfortable, but then he wasn't promised that. The promise was that he would be empowered when he began to act upon his concern. And that's what will happen. It's an absolute guarantee.

Having said, in effect, that those who put their concerns and convictions into action shall be greatly strengthened and encouraged, Jesus now leads us to the third step into the kingdom. "The meek are partakers of the divine blessing," he says, "for they shall inherit the land."

In English, the word "meek" has come to be about the same as "weak" or "harmless" or "spiritless." It is thought that a meek person is something of a doormat upon which everyone wipes his feet, a timid soul who lives in mortal fear of offending his fellow creatures. But nothing could be more foreign to the biblical use of the word. It is used in particular to describe two persons — Moses (Numbers 12:3) and Jesus (Matthew 11:29). One of them defied the might of Egypt and the other couldn't be cowed by a powerful Roman official. Neither of them ever showed the slightest sign of being weak or harmless or spiritless. Both of them seemed absolutely fearless in the face of men, and completely surrendered to the will of God. Can we call them "meek"? The answer is yes.

People may be called "meek" to the extent that they have surrendered their wills to God and learned to do his bidding. The meek won't attempt to explain away God's Word if it goes contrary to their selfish wills. They won't listen to any man, no matter what his power or influence, who tries to make them compromise or disobey their Master's voice. One of the best definitions of meekness in the Bible is the statement of Peter and the other apostles to the Sanhedrin after they had been arrested for preaching about the crucifixion of Jesus: "It's our duty to obey God rather than men" (Acts 5: 29, *Cotton Patch Version*).

It is clear that this is the stuff of which martyrs are made. It is the mysterious ingredient that baffles the high and mighty of this world. They yearn to know its secret. One of them once put his finger on it. Soon after Peter's statement, a member of the Sanhedrin, Gamaliel, stood up and advised the other members: "Stay away from these fellows and let them alone, because if this thing be man's will, it shall fail; but if it be God's will, you won't be able to stop them. *You'll be fighting against God*" (Acts 5:38-39). Right there is the secret to the power of the meek. They surrender their will to God so completely *that God's will becomes their will*. Whoever fights them is fighting against God, for a surrendered human will is the agency through which God's power is released upon the earth. They become God's "workhorses" on earth. Through them his will is done on earth as it is in heaven; through them the kingdom of heaven comes to earth. That's why you can't stop them. That's why they "inherit the land," that is, the promised land or the kingdom. Only the meek, "the terrible meek," the totally committed meek, are considered worthy of an inheritance in the new land, the kingdom of God on earth.

Now let's sum up, and in order to make things a bit clearer, let's compare entering the kingdom to two well-known areas of experience: education and health. In comparing entering the kingdom to entering education, the first three steps would be something like this:

1. *Blessed are they who admit they are ignorant, for theirs is learning.*

2. *Blessed are they who are concerned enough to enroll in school, for they shall be taught.*

3. *Blessed are they who submit to the teacher, for they shall inherit his wisdom.*

Or perhaps we could compare it to entering into health, like this:

1. *Blessed are they who face up to their illness, for theirs is health.*

2. *Blessed are they who go to the doctor, for they shall be helped.*

3. *Blessed are they who take his prescription, for they shall inherit the benefit of his knowledge.*

In the next chapter we shall move on up the ladder into the kingdom. But do not wait until then to take that first step. It's a very low one. Anybody can reach it. The cry, "God, be merciful to me, the sinner," will put you right on it. Take it, now.

# 3 Stairway to Spiritual Life Part 2

"Blessed are they that hunger and thirst after righteousness: for they shall be filled.

"Blessed are the merciful: for they shall obtain mercy.

"Blessed are the pure in heart: for they shall see God.

"Blessed are the peacemakers: for they shall be called sons of God" (Matthew 5:6-9).

In the preceding chapter we found that the Beatitudes were steps into the kingdom, or we might call them stages in the "naturalization" of the kingdom citizen. First, in forsaking his old country, "the world," the spiritual immigrant must feel a deep dissatisfaction with the old citizenship and sense a real need for the new. Second, while recognizing that citizenship is a gift which he could never obtain on his own, he knows that he must be concerned enough to leave the old and make the journey to the new land. Third, when he gets there he must renounce all former allegiances and make a commitment of complete loyalty to the will and way of his adopted country. In the words of the Sermon, he must be "poor in spirit," then a "mourner," and then "meek."

But one must go beyond even the oath of allegiance. Jesus says, "They who hunger and thirst for *the* righteousness are partakers of the divine blessing, for they shall be filled." This is the fourth step into the kingdom. This Beatitude is so important that Jesus felt it necessary to elaborate upon it later in the Sermon. See Matthew 6:1-18. In fact, it might be called the keynote of the whole discourse.

We can understand the Beatitudes better if we recall the prevailing standards of righteousness of Jesus' day. The religious life of the people had become pretty much centered within the temple and the synagogue. It was measured in terms of attendance, contributions, and obedience to the myriad of rules, precepts, traditions, and laws handed down and added to by generations of priests. It was quite professional, and cold, and dignified. Nobody enjoyed it. Like wearing a necktie and coat to church on a hot summer day, it was considered an uncomfortable but necessary thing if you wanted to get along with respectable people.

Two things in particular characterized religious life in Jesus' day. One, it was purely external. People kept the rules because they knew they were expected to, not because they really believed in them. Their righteousness was something like perfume — it wasn't a part of you but if you had it on, it made you smell real sweet. Of course, everybody recognized the odor, but that didn't matter, because they used it, too. Any child could see through the shallow pretense back of it all, but it was a terrible disgrace to let on that you could see through it.

All this quite naturally led to the second characteristic: the motive was reward. Primarily the reward desired was the praise of man. To be well thought of was more highly desired than to be rich. In order to get and hold public approval, a man would sacrifice his own integrity, or perhaps his own son, or his best friend, or even his God. Incredible as it seems, men would even pretend they were serving God in order to please man. We look back upon it and shudder. How could human beings be such hypocrites! And have such nerve! They even expected God to reward them, too. Of course, they weren't nearly so particular about what *he* thought, but they certainly wouldn't go to all the effort and bother to serve him unless they got at least something out of it. They were very much like the elder brother in the parable of the prodigal son: "Look here, all these years I've slaved for you, and never once went contrary to your orders. And yet, at no time have you ever given me so much as a baby goat with which to pitch a party for my friends" (Luke 15:29, *Cotton Patch Version*). It's quite obvious that the motive of this fellow's righteousness was reward, a thing almost as common then as it is today.

Now Jesus was acutely aware of this prevailing hunger and thirst for what everybody called "righteousness" but which in reality was praise. In contrast to this, he felt that kingdom citizens who had really submitted themselves to God would have a deep and genuine desire for the righteousness of the kingdom, instead of a mock hunger for that which had been falsely branded "righteousness." That imitation piety never had satisfied and never would satisfy the inner cravings of the soul. It was like Old Mother Hubbard's cupboard — when you got there it was bare.

Not so with this inward, vital, joyous righteousness rooted in true love of God and man. They who crave it "shall be filled," or better, "shall find it to be satisfying." One might eat and eat of the superficial, cotton-candy righteousness vended by the professional religious hucksters and never have his hunger assuaged. Or he might drink and drink of their holy water and never have his thirst quenched. But the kingdom righteousness is meat indeed and drink indeed — rich, nourishing, satisfying. Blessed are they who hunger and thirst for it, for they shall find that it meets their deepest needs.

The next, and fifth, step into the kingdom grows naturally out of this one. "The merciful are partakers of the divine blessing," Jesus says, "for they shall receive mercy." In the original, the word translated "mercy" certainly means that, but it isn't a cold, condescending kind of mercy such as one in power might extend to his victim in return for gratitude or service. It is warm, compassionate, tender, and never seeks to barter. It is almost exactly the same word that Jesus uses later on in the Sermon in referring to "almsgiving." As we shall see when we study that passage, Jesus rescued the word from the mere act of proudly pitching a coin to a beggar and made it into a whole attitude of life.

By "the merciful" he means *those who have an attitude of such compassion toward all men that they want to share gladly all that they have with one another and with the world.* If they have any money, they don't give till it hurts — they give till it's gone. To them, men are no longer beggars to whom one gives a part, but brothers with whom one shares all. This concept of charity, or mercy, led some of the early Christians to a state of voluntary poverty in which "all the believers were together and held all things in common" (Acts 2:44).

The merciful realize, however, that even though they share their material wealth, regardless of how great it may be, they still have given but little. For they know that while physical needs can be acute, the hunger and thirst of the soul is far greater. They themselves have been through that craving for the righteousness, and they have discovered its amazing power to satisfy. This experience and this knowledge makes them possessors of the true riches. They know a secret. To them a great mystery has been revealed. They have tasted of heaven's manna.

But if they seek to keep their secret, they shall lose it; or if they hoard their manna, it will rot, just as it did for the Israelites in the wilderness (read Exodus 16: 13-20). The one condition of ownership is that it be given away. It is given to each according to the measure with which he shares it. That's why Jesus said, "Blessed are the merciful, *for they shall obtain mercy.*" John senses this when he says, "Whoever has the physical necessities of life and sees his brother standing in need and locks the door of his heart against him, *how can the love of God stay in him?*" (1 John 3:17). God's outreaching love must be well ventilated. It can't live where the doors are closed.

As tragic as it is to show no mercy toward those in physical distress, how much more terrible it is to have the riches of the kingdom and not share with others less fortunate. It is cold cruelty of the worst sort. It would be better to pass by a suffocating man with a tank of oxygen than to pass by a lost person with the keys to the kingdom. For the tragedy is not only what happens to the dying man but also what happens to the one who refuses him life.

We are now ready to take the next step — the sixth one. It's a high one. Jesus says, "The pure in heart are partakers of the divine blessing, for they shall see God." He has said that there must be an honest desire for the real righteousness and that the new life involves sharing it with others, whether they be Jews or Gentiles, Greeks or barbarians, Chinese or Americans. The result of all of this is that *a new nature is formed in us.* We are now pure on the inside, the old selfish nature having been cast out. We are given a righteous nature, which alone is capable of producing righteous deeds. An evil tree *can't* bring forth good fruit. Bad fruit on a bad tree is natural; good fruit on a bad tree is hypocrisy, the worst form of evil. The only remedy is to make the tree good. This is done by giving it a new nature, or making it "pure in heart." Obviously, this purity is not something which man creates himself.

This new nature is a gift from the Father to those who want it and who will receive it and share it. Moreover, as in any other birth, the Father transmits *his own nature* to the child. And of course the new heart that He gives will be a pure one, like his. It will make a clear, decisive, complete break with sin in all its many forms. This break will be followed, not by a wistful longing or even a toleration of the old life, but by an utter abhorrence of it.

There will be a complete break also with one's former masters. If money dictated opinions or governed actions, it will be dethroned and put in its rightful place. Since Mammon is a particularly unruly type of god when he's anywhere except on the throne, it will be necessary in some instances to put him completely outside in order to keep him quiet. The pure in heart, though, won't hesitate to dump him. Nor will they hesitate to dethrone race prejudice, militarism, egotism, or any other of the jealous, demonic gods who demand respect and obedience from the sons of men. They will be the exact opposites of the hypocrites who have two gods — one for the inside and one for the outside.

Now when men attempt to live a double life spiritually, that is, to appear pure on the outside but are not pure in the heart, they are anything but blessed. Their conflicting loyalties make them wretched, confused, tense. And having to keep their eyes on two masters at once makes them cross-eyed, and their vision is so blurred that neither image is clear. But the eyes of the inwardly and outwardly pure are single, that is, focused upon one object, and their sight is not impaired. That's why Jesus said, "For they shall see God." They shall see him because their lives are in focus. All they've got is concentrated on him, and him alone.

This makes it pretty clear, doesn't it, that there is no middle ground in Christianity. The policy of compromise certainly didn't originate in the New Testament. There, lukewarmness is worse than coldness; serving God and Mammon is worse than serving Mammon alone. If one doesn't gather, he scatters; if he isn't for, he's against; if he doesn't love, he hates; if he isn't good, he's evil; if he isn't alive, he's dead. It's a book of radical extremities. From it we get the impression that to be a nominal Christian is more dangerous than to be no Christian. Its central figure seems to step out of its pages and approach the people who bear his name but whose lives are shot through with the adulterating impurities of compromise, and repeat again those strangely familiar and appropriate words: "Blessed are the *pure* in heart, for *they* shall see God." They shall see him *now;* it is not a matter of waiting until we get to heaven.

Yes, they shall see him. They shall see him in his Word, which they will understand as never before. They shall see him in his work, which had been a perplexing riddle to them. They shall see him in his holy temple, the new Israel, the Christian fellowship. But they not only shall see him, *they shall be like him.* "The peacemakers are partakers of the divine blessing, for they shall be called *sons* of God."

It is the Father's nature to make peace. He is called the God of peace. His Son was called the Prince of peace. Paul says, "He *is* our peace." The consuming desire of God seems to have been voiced by the angels at the birth of his Son: ". . . on earth, peace!"

So God the Father is a peacemaker. Quite naturally, little peacemakers, bearing his image, "shall be called sons of God." This final step causes the newborn child to be recognized as a true son, having been begotten of God.

But what is peacemaking? We aren't sure of all that it means, but we can safely say, "It's what God does." And the Bible portrays him as bent on but one thing — the salvation of the world. So we might conclude that a peacemaker is one who identifies himself with God in his plan of redeeming the world. In this way it becomes a Father-son business with a common objective.

With Jesus, peacemaking involved not merely a

change of environment, but also a change of heart. This is shown in how Jesus dealt with an invitation to make peace by settling a dispute between two brothers who were quarreling over the division of their inheritance. But he dismissed the request with the pointed question, "Man, who made me a judge or a divider over you?"

God's plan of making peace is not merely to bring about an outward settlement between evil men, *but to create men of goodwill.*

When Jesus proclaimed the kingdom of God on earth, he was not offering to make men more comfortable in their sins. He was calling them to a new life in the spirit and to citizenship in his beloved community, which alone is capable of peace.

The peacemakers, then, are the agents of the kingdom of heaven. Their assignment is to make "the kingdom of the world become the kingdom of our Lord, and of his Christ" (Revelation 11:15).

# 4 The Effect of the Christian Community on the World

"Blessed are they that have been persecuted for righteousness' sake: for theirs is the kingdom of heaven. Blessed are ye, when *men* shall reproach you, and persecute you, and say all manner of evil against you falsely, for my sake. Rejoice, and be exceedingly glad: for great is your reward in heaven: for so persecuted they the prophets that were before you" (Matthew 5:10-12).
*Read Matthew* 5:10-16.

It is difficult to be indifferent to a wide-awake Christian, a real live son of God. It is even more difficult to be indifferent to a whole body of Christians. You can hate them, or you can love them, but one thing is certain — you can't ignore them. There's something about them that won't let you. It isn't so much what they say or what they do. The thing that seems to haunt you is what they *are*. You can't put them out of your mind any more than you can shake off your shadow.

They confront you with an entirely different way of life, a new way of thinking, a changed set of values, and a higher standard of righteousness. In short, they face you with the kingdom of God on earth, and you have to accept it or reject it. There's no washing of hands. These people must be crowned or crucified, for they are either mighty right or mighty wrong.

To men whose loyalty is to the world, these citizens of the kingdom of heaven are subversive agents, dangerous enemies who must not be tolerated. Jesus, knowing what was in man, anticipated this and spoke to his disciples about it: "They who have endured much for what's right are God's people; they are citizens of His new Order. *You all* are God's people when others call you names, and harass you and tell all kinds of false tales on you just because you follow me. Be cheerful and good-humored, because your spiritual advantage is great. For that's the way they treated men of conscience in the past" (Matthew 5:10-11, *Cotton Patch Version*).

On the surface it might appear that Jesus is saying to his followers, "Go out and get yourselves persecuted, because you won't be real Christians until you do." But this kind of thing leads to a martyr-complex, the basis of which is self-pity. Surely the Master wouldn't say this paid any great spiritual dividends, for he knew that self-pity is a sign of spiritual decay. It will eventually lead a person to persecute himself if he can't get anybody else to do it. He might sleep on a bed of spikes, or walk on hot coals, or if he's in a more civilized country, he might wear a shirt of hurt feelings. It doesn't matter much what hurts him, just so he's hurt and therefore has a legitimate reason to feel sorry for himself. A man's got to suffer for a cause, even if it's just because.

Needless to say, this paganism definitely has no place in Christianity. It was never a part of the thinking of Jesus. Jesus wouldn't even tolerate it, much less commend it.

We must never lose sight of the fact that although Jesus has been accused of being a visionary, he was in truth the world's greatest realist. And you can count on it — he was not blind to the explosive nature of the things he was preaching to the people. It was as clear to him, as it surely must have been to his most casual listener, that his kingdom of spirit and truth was the mortal enemy of systems built on power and greed and oppression and falsehood, and that the two systems could never lie down together. Nobody could have failed to realize that earthshaking conflict was inevitable. Already the storm clouds were gathering, and there was the distant rumble of thunder in a supercharged atmosphere. Would he let the fury of it burst upon their terrified hearts with no word of calm assurance from him? Never! He would speak to them as a mother who gathers her child in her arms and presses its pounding heart to hers.

Now as we have already seen, he didn't tell the people to go out and see if they could make the storm a bit worse. Nor did he try to comfort them by telling them that it really wasn't a storm at all — just a lot of lightning and thunder and rain and wind — and that they needn't worry because if they would just leave it all up to him, he would take care of everything. He did not say that they should try to get to sleep, because when they would wake up the sun would be shining. He just was not that naïve, nor were they that gullible. Besides, they were all grown men, and childish prattle had little appeal for them.

It seems to me that he said something like this: "Fellows, this is it. You think you've already been through a lot. You're just getting started. As you walked up these steps and came into my kingdom, I made it clear to you that you were thereby making an all-out commitment. I charge you now to be faithful to it, cost what it may.

But don't let them scare you or bully you or make you back down. Rejoice that you've been counted worthy to be on our side. You're in a great company of prophets whose glorious past stretches back to the beginning of time and whose future has no end. So go to it. I'm with you."

A modern illustration of what Jesus meant is given by E. T. Thompson in his book, *The Sermon on the Mount.* He says that Dr. Turner, who was pastor of the American Church in Berlin before World War II, visited Pastor Heinrich Niemoeller, the aged father of Martin Niemoeller who defied Hitler and spent many months in a concentration camp. When the visit was over, they stood at the door, talking. Dr. Turner continued: "Grandmother Niemoeller held my left hand in her two hands. The grandfather of Martin's seven children patted my right hand and then put one hand on my shoulder. 'When you go back to America,' he said slowly, 'do not let anyone pity the father and mother of Martin Niemoeller. Only pity any follower of Christ who does not know the joy that is set before those who endure the cross despising the shame. Yes, it is a terrible thing to have a son in a concentration camp,' the aged man concluded. 'Paula here and I know that. But there would be something more terrible for us: if God had needed a faithful martyr, and our Martin had been unwilling.'" That's about the gist of what Jesus said. Persecution is a terrible thing, but unfaithfulness is far worse.

We may go further. The history of the Christian movement demonstrates that the intensity of persecution is geared, not to the moral level of the non-Christians, or persecutors, but to the intensity of the witness of the Christian community. The early believers were not persecuted because the Romans were such bad people. In fact, according to the world's standards, they were quite decent. Oh, on big occasions they would throw a thousand or two helpless people into the amphitheater to be clawed to pieces by lions, but the thought of atomizing a whole city probably would have horrified them. The strong convictions of the believers might not have *caused* the Romans to persecute them, but there could have been no persecution without such a faith. One wonders why Christians today get off so easily. Is it because unchristian Americans are that much better than unchristian Romans, or is our light so dim that the tormentor can't see it? What are the things we do that are worth persecuting?

Well, it might sound like meddling, but Jesus has something to say about that, too. "You folks are the world's salt, but now if the salt loses its strength [the Greek word is "to be foolish, to act foolishly"; we get our word "moron" from this Greek form], what shall the world use for salt?" Jesus says, "After that, it isn't good for a thing except to fill up mud puddles in the road." In Luke he says, "Salt is mighty good, but if it, too, becomes flat, how shall it be seasoning? It isn't fit for the land or even for the compost heap. People throw it away." (See Luke 14:34.)

It's hard to see how anybody could miss the meaning of such pointed words as those. Yet some people insist on putting a period after "Ye are the salt of the earth," and strut about as though Jesus said nothing else. They turn into a compliment what he intended as a dire warning. He did not call his followers salt to describe

them or to point out their saving and savoring abilities
— he did that with the Beatitudes. He called them salt
for but one purpose — *to warn them that they can lose
their power to salt.* When this happens, men will no
longer bother to persecute Christians. They'll do something even worse; they'll dump them out and go on
about their business.

Whenever tension ceases to exist between the church
and the world, one of two things has happened: Either
the world has been completely converted to Christ and
his Way, or the church has watered down and compro-
mised its original heritage. In the latter position, the
church, due to its weakness, loses its influence and is
discarded.

The history of the Christian church is full of illustrations of this truth. One of the more recent ones is the
way the church was booted out of Russia after the revolution. The priesthood was utterly corrupt, and the
church sought to maintain the *status quo* by siding with
the Czarist regime against the exploited masses. Church
officials clearly sold the Christian birthright for a mess
of pottage. The salt lost its strength, and when the
revolution came, the salt was promptly cast out. Or,
to use another graphic scriptural illustration of this
truth, "I know your works: you are neither cold nor hot.
Would that you were cold or hot! So, because you are
lukewarm, and neither cold nor hot, I will spew you
out of my mouth" (Revelation 3:15-16, RSV).

That church is yet to be found which long survived
in the midst of race prejudice, national pride, militarism, and exploitation without lifting up a mighty
"Thus saith the Lord." To be sure, when it so speaks,

it becomes a persecuted church, but it is always so virile that men find extreme difficulty in ignoring it or trampling it under foot.

In fact, Jesus says it can't be done. "It is impossible to hide a city that's situated on a hill." By this figure Jesus means that when the Father created the Christian community, he never had any intentions of locating it in the sheltered cove but on a windswept hilltop where it might be an eternal witness to the way men should live. His next figure says the same thing in different words: "People don't light a lamp and put it under a bushel basket, but upon the lampstand, and it shines on all those that are in the house" (Matthew 5:15).

Jesus isn't saying here that you shouldn't hide your light. He says that nobody *ever* does that. Now if *people* don't ever light a lamp and hide it, neither does *God*. The Christian community is his light which he has lit up with the glory of his own Son, and he has no intention of hiding it. When we come into the fellowship, we become a part of that light. While we can determine the intensity of it, we cannot escape the fact that we are part of the witness, for better or for worse. It is not a matter of whether or not we will shine, but how. Jesus says it should be in such a manner "that men might see your lovely ways and give the credit to your spiritual Father" (Matthew 5:16).

"That men might *see* your lovely *ways*. . . ." Why did he tack an uncomfortable thing like that on to a nice compliment like "Ye are the light of the world"? How nice it would have been if he had said, "That men might hear your wonderful preacher," or "that they might see your beautiful new sanctuary," or "hear your choir," or "see your financial report," or "read a copy of those strong resolutions you adopted." Yet he didn't say it that way. And with his simple words he placed the church under an eternal obligation to *live its message,* cost what it may.

Of course, the church must also preach the Word, but at the same time realize that the power of the spoken word lies in the demonstration of it. It must be an expression of an experience in which the whole fellowship participates. The preacher alone cannot bear witness to the Christian message; the whole congregation bears the testimony. *It* is the light of the world; *it* is the city situated upon a hill. Therefore, by the way in which the Christian fellowship lives is the gospel of Christ made known to the world. Thus every member of the body is a part of the witness, either strengthening it or weakening it.

Since we can't escape shining, since we cannot be hid, our testimony should be a credit to the Father. We must not live as cowardly, cringing weaklings. Whether persecution or praise be our lot is immaterial. The main thing is that men may clearly see in us the image of the Father who begot us, and that we may be the kind of sons and daughters in whom the Father is well pleased. For the world has no way of seeing God except through the image of Christ which is formed in the hearts of those who love and obey him.

If you wish to be a part of this great witness, you must come into the fellowship and join the forces of light in their warfare against darkness. A lone Christian is not a city set upon a hill, nor will his single candle light the world. You need your brothers, and they need you. Your gifts or your goodwill won't suffice. You must give yourself and take your stand with Christ's people, thereby increasing the candlepower of the light of the world.

If you are already in the fellowship, you should work unceasingly to keep it true to the whole gospel of Jesus Christ. You should see that your personal life and conduct cause no dimming of the light. With unflinching courage you should seek to eliminate all barriers to genuine fellowship until men *know* that you are Christ's disciples because you love one another. And above all, you should urge and encourage all men everywhere to forsake their evil, selfish ways and to come into the kingdom, that they, too, might be a part of the light of the world, citizens of the holy city.

# 5 Things New and Old, Part 1

"Think not that I came to destroy the law or the prophets: I came not to destroy, but to fulfill" (Matthew 5:17).

"But I say unto you, that every one that looketh on a woman to lust after her hath committed adultery with her already in his heart" (Matthew 5:28).

"But let your speech be, Yea, yea; Nay, nay: and whatsoever is more than these is of the evil *one*" (Matthew 5:37).

*Read Matthew* 5:17-20; 27-37.

Many people of the first century considered Jesus a lawbreaker. He didn't observe the sabbath in keeping with their pet theories (Mark 2:23–3:6). He seemed to disregard rules about fasting (Mark 2:18). He openly defied the time-honored traditions of ceremonial cleansing of hands and cups and plates before eating (Mark 7:1-5). To people who placed the rules of etiquette above the Ten Commandments, he was a dangerous criminal. And in their thinking the worst thing he did was to associate with low-class people and actually to *eat* with them (Luke 15:1). Judged by Pharisaic standards, which were commonly accepted, he had no breeding, was impolite, uncouth, impious, and irreligious.

Since Jesus did not plan to establish his kingdom communities in monasteries on lonely islands, he needed to help his believers to understand their relationship to their world. Obviously he was beginning a new society, a new world order. But what were its connections with the old? Was everything in the old life to be thrown overboard when the new was accepted? Was there any point of contact between the kingdom and Judaism? Had all the faithfulness and sacrifice and suffering of Moses and the prophets and the people been futile? No doubt these were some questions which perplexed believers and nonbelievers alike.

It was characteristic of Jesus to face them squarely. "Don't think," he said, "that I came to do away with the law or the prophets. I didn't come to pervert them but to pervade them. Indeed, I'm telling you, until heaven and earth pass away, not one comma or period shall be dropped from the law until it all comes to pass." Now it should be pointed out that when Jesus referred to the Law, he was speaking of the written law of the Old Testament and not the oral traditions and interpretations of the rabbis which to them had come to be as sacred and binding as the original. He wanted the people to understand that he had no quarrel with the Law itself. He did take issue, however, with the ecclesiastical perversions of it. His desire was to show the real spirit which pervaded the Law and to point out the purpose for which it existed. He felt that the people had been led astray from the original intent. It was really they and not he who were out of step with God. The kingdom movement was really a "restoration of Israel."

But what was the intent of the Law? Simply this: to cause people to live together in peace and harmony with one another and with God. The Israelites had emerged from Egypt as a motley mob of liberated slaves, and it was God's desire that they be welded into a united, harmonious, cooperative community. This could not be done if every man were a law unto himself. The welfare of the individual and that of the whole had to be considered together. So God gave them laws which defined these relationships and made it possible for them to live together without getting in each other's hair. If a person insisted upon having his own way, to the detriment of the common welfare, the Law provided for pressure, or penalties, which could be applied to him. Under these circumstances he might lose sight of the original intent of the Law and be motivated by fear of the consequences of breaking it. Such a person would be scrupulous to obey the letter of the Law without seeing the spirit of it. To him, the Law would be a fearful, external mold into which he must pour himself.

Now Jesus said that was the wrong attitude to have toward it. The whole Law and Prophets, he said, were aiming at but one thing, and what was to get people to love the Lord their God with all their heart and with all their soul and with all their mind, and to love their neighbors as themselves (Matthew 22:37-40). And he said he wasn't going to drop one comma or period from the Law until it reached this objective. The purpose of the Law was not to enslave men but to lead them to the freedom which only love can produce.

He knew in his soul that the scribes and Pharisees would never fulfill the Law in the way they were going about it. He warned, "Except your righteousness goes beyond that of the scribes and Pharisees, you'll never get into the kingdom of heaven." They had lost their sense of direction and made the Law an end within itself.

They were treading water in an ethical sea. The hope of reaching harbor had been replaced by an involuntary impulse just to keep their souls afloat.

Their (the scribes' and Pharisees') righteousness concerned itself with reputation; Jesus made character the basis of kingdom righteousness. Theirs revolved around the act; his around the attitude. Theirs was external; his was internal. They did it to be seen of men; he said only the Father should know about it. They placed obedience above love; he felt that obedience would naturally grow out of love. They made law the cold, unbending, structural steel of society; he knew that it was aimed at a new society of love where men might grow so strong that law would be unnecessary. The mark of their righteousness was hypocrisy; the mark of his was sincerity and purity. They would try to make the tree good by making its fruit good; he would make the tree good and let the fruit take care of itself. They set up the double standard of justice for others and mercy for themselves; he held to the single standard of doing unto others as you would have them do unto you.

To show how the kingdom citizen really did not break the Law but kept it, and how the kingdom righteousness went far beyond the prevailing standards, Jesus used a number of illustrations. He called attention to some of the old laws — the laws against murder, against adultery, against oaths, and regarding retaliation. He held them up for examination in the light of the kingdom standard. In this chapter we shall deal with the laws concerning adultery and oaths, and discuss murder and retaliation in the next chapter.

"You learned that it was commanded: 'Thou shalt not commit adultery.' But I am saying to you that any man who looks a woman over with a lustful longing for her is an adulterer at heart" (Matthew 5:27-28). According to the Pharisaic interpretation of the Law, a person was not guilty of transgression until he committed the act. He might be ever so lustful and even justify and encourage adultery, but so long as neither circumstances nor opportunity allowed him to do the actual deed, he was still safely righteous. It was about like chaining a vicious dog to a tree and saying that because he had never bitten anyone he was a good dog. The extent of his goodness, however, would be dependent upon the strength of the chain.

To Jesus, the Law was like that chain. It was a good thing for keeping vicious people in check. But there would be no violation of the chain's purpose if someone tamed the dog and made him so gentle that a chain was unnecessary. Even so, Jesus felt that he was in keeping with the Law when he insisted that his subjects have a nature so clean and pure that they wouldn't need the Law. It just wouldn't be in their nature to commit the act.

In the light of this, let's examine what Jesus had to say about adultery. He did not say that everyone who had a sexual impulse was an adulterer at heart. That would have condemned every normal person. This was no puritanical rebuke of every thought of sex. He was simply saying that there is no difference between the act of adultery and the willingness to commit it. When a person approves of it and justifies it and then looks lustfully at the opposite sex, that person is an adulterer even though he has not actually engaged in the sexual act. So the normal sex impulse of healthy people is not evil if it is kept under complete control. But you'd better watch out when you lower your standards and ideals and start telling yourself it's perfectly all right to indulge in immoral relations. That's a sure sign of the lustful nature which will produce the deed at the first opportunity.

This is what Jesus meant when he said, "So if your right eye ensnares you, cut it out and throw it away, because it's better that one of your organs perish than the whole body be thrown into Gehenna. And if your right hand ensnares you, cut it off and throw it away, because it is better that one of your members perish than the whole body be carried off to Gehenna" (Matthew 5:29-30).* The eye and the hand are God-given organs to be used in the service of the whole body. But if somehow they should become infected and endanger one's life, they should be promptly sacrificed. Jesus felt that the same principle should be applied to the sex instinct. Even though it is God-given, if it should become perverted and endanger the whole personality, it should be ruthlessly sacrificed. To bring the sex instinct under control and deny it free expression might be as

*Gehenna was a valley outside Jerusalem where refuse was burned, corresponding perhaps to our city garbage dump. Dr. Jordan points out that Gehenna was originally the site where little children were burned as a sacrifice to Moloch. Thayer says, "The Jews so abhorred the place after these horrible sacrifices had been abolished by King Josiah, that they cast into it not only all manner of refuse, but even the dead bodies of animals and of unburied criminals who had been executed. And since fires were always needed to consume the dead bodies, that the air might not become tainted by their putrefaction, it came to pass that the place was called Gehenna of fire." Dr. Jordan prefers as a translation the modern word "incinerator" or "city garbage burner."

painful as plucking out an eye or chopping off a hand. But this is nothing compared to the hell of fire which burns the whole personality of those who do not exercise such discipline. And they who are burning will be the first to admit that this is true.

The next words of Jesus are so clear as to hardly need comment. "It was said, 'Whoever divorces his wife, let him give her written evidence.' But I'm telling you that everyone who divorces his wife except for fornication makes her an adulteress, and whoever marries a divorcee commits adultery."* Here was the situation: Lustful men fretted at the law against adultery, which chained their appetites. Then the happy thought occurred to them that there was no law against *marrying* the object of their lust. The problem, though, was what to do with such a wife when you got tired of her and wanted another. Well, in that case you'd have to unmarry her, but in order to keep her reputation clean you should give her written evidence that she was no longer married to you. Jesus just bluntly called all this finagling by its proper name — legalized adultery. Marriage or no marriage, they were breaking the real intent of the law which was aimed at preserving the sacredness of the home.

Jesus next used the law concerning oaths to illustrate how his righteousness went beyond that of the scribes and Pharisees. "Again you have heard that it was said to the old-timers, 'You shall not overswear, but you shall deliver your oaths to the Lord.' But I tell you,

*In Luke 16:18, where the same verse occurs, "except for fornication" is omitted. There is some evidence that this was not originally a part of Matthew's text.

don't swear by anything at all; neither by the heaven just because it is God's throne, nor by the earth because it is a footstool for his feet, nor by Jerusalem because it is the city of the Great King. You shouldn't even swear by your head, because you can't make one hair white or black. But let your word be a simple 'yes' or 'no.' If it's more than that, it's bad" (Matthew 5:33-37) .

Now what was the purpose of this law about oaths? The purpose was to help men become more truthful. An oath was an external cord which bound a man to his word, and the Law said that he should never break it. But at times it wasn't convenient or pleasant or profitable to hold to one's word. Yet the Law must be obeyed. What could be done?

Well, here's what they did. They admitted that an oath should be binding, but then they said that it should be no more binding than the thing sworn by. In other words, your word should be dependent upon your collateral. If you swore by a trifling thing, such as a hair on your head, of course your oath would not be as binding as if you swore by your whole head. And if you swore by the earth, which is merely God's footstool, it wasn't nearly as serious as swearing by heaven, which is his throne. Now the main point, they said, was not to overswear, that is, to swear by something bigger than the oath really called for. Always try to get the one to whom you swear to accept as little collateral as possible so as to reduce to the minimum the binding effect of the oath. When you have done that, then you should turn over the contract to the Lord for his approval. In other words, all oaths should be binding only "if the Lord wills." Then in case you want to break one, you can always say the Lord didn't will it. This leaves you free from guilt, and quite naturally no one would accuse the Lord of dealing falsely. So if you were really careful, you could maintain a spotless reputation for truthfulness and honesty.

Thus a law that was designed to encourage truthfulness was actually being used to foster lying. Jesus told them to cut out all the shenanigans and to attach no conditions whatever to their word. "Yes" should mean yes and "no" should mean no. If it was any other way, it came from an evil, conniving nature that was essentially dishonest and whose word would not be any good anyway, even though it were placed on top of a whole stack of Bibles. Jesus wanted it understood that his kingdom would not consist of a bunch of rules and regulations imposed on evil men in order to make them behave themselves. He knew that they had lawyers and some of them would always be smart enough to wiggle around any set of rules. With him, if a man wasn't honest on the inside, he wasn't honest. His kingdom called not for a change of law but for a change of heart.

And this call is the same today. The Father is seeking for those who will worship him in spirit and in truth, for they alone are eligible for kingdom citizenship. They are the material out of which he can build a new heaven and a new earth wherein dwelleth righteousness. Are you willing for him to use you?

# 6 Things New and Old, Part 2

"Ye have heard that it was said to them of old time, Thou shalt not kill; and whosoever shall kill shall be in danger of the judgment: but I say unto you, that every one who is angry with his brother shall be in danger of the judgment; and whosoever shall say to his brother, Raca, shall be in danger of the council; and whosoever shall say, Thou fool, shall be in danger of the hell of fire" (Matthew 5:21-22).
*Read Matthew 5:21-26.*

Life in the Christian brotherhood calls for a much higher standard of righteousness than an external code of "dos" and "don'ts." With Jesus, the *way* a person did a thing and *why* he did it were as important as *what* he did. The motive and the deed were inseparable. He knew that man would never solve the problem of moral behavior by changing outward rules; man's heart would have to change.

The surest way to insure the keeping of the law against murder, for example, is to develop within a person a peaceful disposition. "You learned that it was said to the old-timers, 'You shall not murder,' and also, 'whosoever murders shall be subject to the death penalty,' (Exodus 21:12); but I'm saying to you that everyone who has an attitude of anger toward his brother*

*The Revised Standard Version correctly omits "without cause" which appears in the King James Version.

shall be subject to the death penalty; and whoever says to his brother, 'Harrka' shall be subject to the court, and whoever says, 'You idiot,' shall be subject to Gehenna" (Matthew 5:21-22).

The verses are fairly clear, except for the name-calling. What did it mean to say "Harrka" to someone, and what was so terrible about it? The word is an effort to give the sound of a person harking and clearing his throat to spit. When the Jew wanted to express his utter contempt for someone, he would spit on him, usually in his face. This was considered about the meanest thing you could do to a person, and we can certainly understand why. To call anyone an idiot was equally bad. And people took it more seriously then than they do now. The term cast reflection upon the person about whom it was spoken; it indicated that the speaker didn't have a very high estimate of his brother. So both of these terms were expressions of a low evaluation of one's fellowman and a readiness to treat him as less than human.

Jesus is saying, then, that murder really begins when one loses his respect for human personality and the infinite worth of every individual. When a man spits in the face of his brother and looks with contempt upon him because of his race or some other fictitious difference, he has in his heart a spirit which may result in murder. The foundation of slavery in America was disrespect for the individual worth of Africans. The Nazi concentration camps and death chambers of World War II sprang from a contempt for the Jews. This basic contempt expresses itself today in race prejudice which cause segments of the population to be slowly murdered in body and soul by the slums. When one says "nigger," or "wop," or "chink," he is more of a murderer than he realizes.

If a person convinces himself that the lives of others aren't worth much, the inference is drawn that it does not matter particularly what happens to them. They may be shot, they may be exploited or bombed, or they may be used as cannon fodder, and it's perfectly all right. Nations do it, of course, on the wholesale and not just one at a time. Thus "Harrka," or contempt, leads to a justification of murder and this makes one a murderer at heart.

It was to this that Jesus was referring when he spoke of being angry with one's brother. He did not mean the occasional fit of temper which might sweep over one. The word that he used originally meant to teem, or swell, and referred especially to the internal swelling of plants and fruits with juice. Then it came to be used to describe a person who boiled up on the inside until he was ready to explode. So he is talking about those who are swelling with anger, who have a mounting, growing disposition or attitude of anger and hate and malice toward their brothers. Such people find it increasingly difficult to get along with others. Having a murderous nature, they are, according to Jesus, subject to the death penalty.

Whether it be anger or contempt, the terrible consequences are visited not so much upon the victims as upon the person exercising these traits. "Death penalty," "subject to the Sanhedrin" (remember what this Jewish court did to Jesus?), "into the Gehenna of fire" — these are strong words to warn of the devastating effects which anger and contempt have upon the personality, and even upon the body. Today's physicians and psychiatrists would agree; they know that one cannot live with an attitude of swelling anger any more than one can endure a growing tumor. In time, both will prove to be fatal.

One of the early signs of a disposition of anger is self-pity with its attendant hurt feelings. Craving attention, and not getting as much as you think you should, you become angry and seek to punish those withholding affection from you by making them feel they have hurt you in some way. You sulk and pout and become resentful. This leads to another sign, that of withdrawal.

When you find yourself getting into this mess, it's time to take immediate action. Listen to what Jesus says! "If you are offering your gift upon the altar" (the disposition of anger will frequently withdraw and seek solace in religion), "and there you remember that your brother has something against you, leave your gift there before the altar and go out and first get right with your brother and then come back and make your offering" (Matthew 5:23-24). That's really the only hope for you. The worst thing possible would be to attempt to escape from facing up to your real situation by crying on God's shoulder. He'll have none of it — for *your* benefit. He wants you to stop thinking you have grounds for being mad at other people; it's probably the other way around. Take the initiative in getting things put right. You'll be amazed at how much better you and God will get along. Your offering, as well as your whole religious life, will be a joyous thing. Incidentally, you won't be as apt to be bothered with high blood pressure and stomach ulcers.

57

Of course, it might not be easy to get right with some people. You might honestly be like the fellow who was testifying in a meeting and said, "The Lord, he done saved me and blessed me. And I love him and intend to follow him. And I love all the brethren, but I want to say right here there's a few of them that I ain't no fool about." But even if your enemy should be a vicious adversary, Jesus advises, "Be agreeable with your opponent quickly while you are with him in a difficulty, lest he take you before the judge, and the judge turn you over to the jailer, and you be put in the prison. I'm telling you a fact — you won't get out of there until you've paid the last cent of your fine" (Matthew 5: 25-26).

Please note that Jesus did not say, *"Agree* with thine adversary," as the King James translation has it, but *"be* agreeable." His emphasis was on the attitude. He was fully aware that there would be many times when the kingdom citizen would find himself in complete disagreement with the opinions and actions of people of the world, and that this could easily lead one to be cross, angry, and generally disagreeable. This was what Henry Ward Beecher had in mind when he said, "I can stand reforms, but I can't stomach reformers." People who are right are usually in the greatest danger of being a nuisance. The fact that they are right, and know it, has a powerful tendency to make them intolerant of those who are not in a position to see it their way. And this further alienates the very people who need to be drawn closer. Truth is thus hurt by its own advocates.

In this way the kingdom, too, could suffer at the hands of its own citizens. If Christians make themselves disagreeable and objectionable by forcing their doctrines and beliefs (however right they may be) upon other people (however wrong they may be), they hurt not only themselves but the cause and truth they represent — the kingdom itself. So for the kingdom's sake, be agreeable with those who oppose you and it.

As with anger and contempt, the one who is hurt the most by a disagreeable disposition is the one who has it. It leads to a progressive imprisonment of the soul — "lest he take you before the judge, and the judge turn you over to the jailer, and you be put in prison." Like the creeping tentacles of an octopus, it lays hold of the personality and destroys its freedom. Booker T. Washington sensed this debasing effect when he said, "I will allow no man to drag me so low as to make me hate him." Having come out of slavery, he had felt the sting of hate and prejudice, but he had also learned Jesus' great truth that he who holds the whip is hurt far more than the one who is beaten. Perhaps this is what John had in mind when he said, "If anyone enslaves, he is on his way to slavery; if anyone kills with a sword, he is bound to be killed with a sword. In this truth lies the steadfastness and faith of the believers" (Revelation 13:10). So not only for the kingdom's sake but also for your own sake, be agreeable with your adversary.

An illustration of how this truth works out is revealed in a story related by an old colonel in the Austrian army.

"I was commanded," the old colonel began, "to march against a little town in the Tyrol and lay siege to it. We had been meeting stubborn resistance in that part of the country, but we felt sure that we should win because all of the advantages were on our side. My confidence, however, was arrested by a remark from a prisoner we had taken. 'You will never take that town,' he said, 'for they have an invincible leader.'

" 'What does the fellow mean?' I inquired of one of my staff. 'And who is this leader of whom he speaks?'

"Nobody seemed able to answer my question, and so in case there should be some truth in the report, I doubled preparations.

"As we descended through the pass in the Alps, I saw with surprise that the cattle were still grazing in the valley and that women and children — yes, and even men — were working in the fields.

" 'Either they are not expecting us, or this is a trap to catch us,' I thought to myself. As we drew nearer the town we passed people on the road. They smiled and greeted us with a friendly word, and then went on their way.

"Finally we reached the town and clattered up the cobble-paved streets — colors flying, horns sounding a challenge, arms in readiness. Women came to the windows or doorways with little babies in their arms. Some of them looked startled and held the babies closer, then went quietly on with their household tasks without panic or confusion. It was impossible to keep strict discipline, and I began to feel rather foolish. My soldiers answered the questions of the children, and I saw one old warrior throw a kiss to a little golden-haired tot on a doorstep. 'Just the size of my Lisa,' he muttered. Still no sign of an ambush. We rode straight to the open square which faced the town hall. Here, if anywhere, resistance surely was to be expected.

"Just as I had reached the hall and my guard was drawn up at attention, an old white-haired man, who by his insignia I surmised to be the mayor, stepped forth, followed by ten men in simple peasant costume. They were all dignified and unabashed by the armed force before them — the most terrible soldiers of the great and mighty army of Austria.

"He walked down the steps straight to my horse's side, and with hand extended, cried, 'Welcome, brother!' One of my aides made a gesture as if to strike him down with his sword, but I saw by the face of the old mayor that this was no trick on his part.

" 'Where are your soldiers?' I demanded.

" 'Soldiers? Why, don't you know we have none?' he replied in wonderment, as though I had asked, 'Where are your giants,' or 'Where are your dwarfs?'

" 'But we have come to take this town.'

" 'Well, no one will stop you.'

" 'Are there none here to fight?'

"At this question, the old man's face lit up with a rare smile that I will always remember. Often afterward, when engaged in bloody warfare, I would suddenly see that man's smile — and somehow, I came to hate my business. His words were simply:

" 'No, there is no one here to fight. We have chosen Christ for our Leader, and he taught men another way.'

"There seemed nothing left for us to do but to ride away, leaving the town unmolested. It was impossible to take it. If I had ordered my soldiers to fire on those smiling men, women, and children, I knew they would not have obeyed me. Even military discipline has its limits. Could I command the grisly soldier to shoot down the child who reminded him of his Lisa? I reported to headquarters that the town had offered unassailable resistance, although this admission injured my military reputation. But I was right. We had literally been conquered by these simple folk who followed implicitly the leadership of Jesus Christ."*

Now let's sum up. The Law said not to commit the deed of murder. But Jesus said we mustn't stop there but we must go on behind the act to the motive or the nature. With him, a wrathful and contemptuous attitude was as much a part of murder as the actual killing. Such a nature carried with it its own terrible punishment. To escape it, the one having this disposition must not hide it under a religious covering but must take the initiative and be reconciled with his brother. Naturally this will involve throwing overboard wrath and contempt. From then on he must cultivate an agreeable disposition. This will intensify his witness to the way of the kingdom, will enrich his own life and strengthen his character, and will "redeem" rather than destroy his adversary.

In the next chapter we'll see how Jesus goes into even greater detail and shows how this course of action is in keeping with the nature of the Father himself.

*Condensed from *The Friendly Story Caravan* by Anna Pettit Broomell. Published by J. B. Lippincott Co., and used by permission.

# 7 Things New and Old, Part 3

"Ye have heard that it was said, An eye for an eye, and a tooth for a tooth: but I say unto you, Resist not him that is evil: but whosoever smiteth thee on thy right cheek, turn to him the other also" (Matthew 5:38-39).

"Ye have heard that it was said, Thou shalt love thy neighbor, and hate thine enemy: but I say unto you, Love your enemies, and pray for them that persecute you" (Matthew 5:43-44).

*Read Matthew* 5:38-48.

We have seen that Jesus thought of the Mosaic laws as disciplines or steps toward the creation of a new society made up of new people. His proclamation of the kingdom of heaven did not destroy the Law but fulfilled it, just as the fruit of a tree does not destroy the blossom but fulfills it, that is, brings it to its highest culmination. Jesus climaxed this thought by pointing out the stages through which the law of retaliation had passed, and how it finally came to rest in the universal love of the Father's own heart.

There were four of these steps, each clearly defined and each progressing toward God's final purpose. First, there was the way of *unlimited retaliation;* second, that of *limited retaliation;* third, that of *limited love;* and fourth, that of *unlimited love.* Let us seek to discover the meaning of each of these steps on the road from retaliation to reconciliation.

The first method of dealing with one's enemies was that of unlimited retaliation. According to this principle, if somebody knocked out one of your eyes, you were justified in knocking out both of his, if you could get to him. If any enemy knocked out one of your teeth, you could knock out his whole set, if you were able. There was no limit placed on revenge. It was the law of the jungle; every man for himself. Like beasts, men would return a bite for a snarl. This philosophy might be expressed thus, "Kill my dog, I'll kill your cat; kill my cat, I'll kill your cow; kill my cow, I'll kill your mule; kill my mule, I'll kill you." It's the same kind of stuff that some civilized, modern nations use today in fanning a minor incident into a full-scale war. The daddy of this idea is the theory that "might makes right." If one has the power to inflict more injury than he receives, he has the right to do so. The main thing is to make sure ahead of time that you have more strength than your enemy. Of course, all the while he'll be making an effort to have more power than you, but it will be a lively contest, even though there might not be any survivors.

It became evident that the end result of this method would be mutual self-destruction. Therefore, a better way was sought, and the law of limited retaliation arose. This principle declared that if one harmed another, "then thou shalt give life for life, eye for eye, tooth for tooth, hand for hand, foot for foot, burning for burning, wound for wound, stripe for stripe." (See Exodus 21:23-25; also Leviticus 24:20; Deuteronomy 19:21.) According to this law, if one knocks out one of your eyes, you must not knock out *both* of his, just one. Or if it's a tooth, you must not retaliate by knocking out *all* of his teeth, just one. In other words, limit your retaliation to the exact amount of the injury. Get even, but no more. Do unto others as they do unto you. This is the attitude that characterizes some modern business organizations. The books must exactly balance, penny for penny, dollar for dollar. It's also what many people have in mind when they speak of "justice." It is the most frequent basis of capital punishment.

Now limited retaliation is a sight better than unlimited retaliation, especially if you're on the receiving end, but Jesus felt that kingdom citizens should go further yet. He said, "You've also heard the saying, 'Take an eye for an eye; take a tooth for a tooth.' But I'm telling you, *never* respond with evil. Instead, if somebody slaps you on your right cheek, offer him the other one too. And if anybody wants to drag you into court and take away your shirt, let him have your undershirt. If somebody makes you go a mile for him, go two miles. Give to him who asks of you, and don't turn your back on anyone who wants a loan" (Matthew: 5:38-42, *Cotton Patch Version*). All this adds up to one thing: Let yourself be imposed upon.

The third stage is that of limited love. This method is prescribed in the Old Testament and is referred to by Jesus when he said, "All of you have heard that it was said, 'Love your neighbor and hate your enemy'" (Leviticus 19:18). Some devout Jews might have agreed with Jesus that if your neighbor, i.e., another Jew, knocked out your eye or tooth he might possibly be forgiven, but if he were an enemy, i.e., a Gentile, then he should be given the works. The idea was that there had to be *some* limit to this love and goodwill business, and the proper place to draw the line was with your own race. In this way a man could have two standards of righteousness: one in dealing with his kinsmen and another in dealing with strangers. This is what happens invariably in a biracial society when the minority group is fairly large. It is the bulwark of prejudice and is echoed in such cries as "white supremacy" and "Herrenvolk." It is also manifested in nationalism, which is merely another form of prejudice, and is back of such slogans as "America for the Americans," not meaning, naturally, the original Americans, the Indians.

To be sure, love, even though limited to one's own circle, is far superior to retaliation, whether limited or unlimited. But Jesus didn't feel that even this brought the law to its final goal, or fulfillment. It was making progress, but would not be complete until it arrived at unlimited love. "But I'm telling you, love the outsiders and pray for those who try to do you in, so that you might be sons of your spiritual Father. For he lets his sun rise on both sinners and saints, and he sends rain on both good people and bad. Listen here, if you love only those who love you, what is your advantage? Don't even scalawags do that much? And if you speak to no one but your friends, how are you any different? Do not the non-Christians do as much? Now you, you all must be mature, as your spiritual Father is mature" (Matthew 5:44-48, *Cotton Patch Version*).

Here Jesus is simply saying that, for kingdom citizens, love must be the basis of all relationships and that it must be applied universally, both to one's race and nation and to those of other races and nations. There must be no double-dealing, no two-facedness, no partiality. Hate has the same effect upon the personality whether its object is friend or foe. Spiritual traffic cannot be halted at the artificial borders of caste or nation.

Some people rise up to say that this just isn't practical. It might be all right to turn the other cheek to a little baby enemy that can't hit very hard anyway, but it just won't work with a big, bad, grown-up enemy who might knock the daylights out of you. Force is the only language some people can understand (and the only language some people can speak!) so you might as well be realistic about the matter. Suppose you try to be nice to everybody and give to those who ask of you and lend to those who borrow and let the guy who takes the shirt off your back have your undershirt, too, and then they take advantage of you. With human nature being what it is, can you go in for this until everybody is willing to live that way?

Then there are people who say that this attitude is very practical and will work if given a chance. They believe that even in the most cruel person there's a tender spot which will respond to a continuous bombardment of love and goodwill.

Citing many examples from history, they can present a strong case for the effectiveness of nonretaliation and active love. Many of them are willing to back up their belief in this idea with their lives, which within itself is a strong argument.

The truth might be that in its initial stages unlimited love is very impractical. Folks who are determined enough to hold on to it usually wind up on a cross, like Jesus. Their goods get plundered and they get slandered. Persecution is their lot. Surely nobody would be inclined to call this practical. Yet in its final stages, unlimited love seems to be the only thing that can possibly make any sense. Crucifixions have a way of being followed by resurrections. The end of love seems to be its beginning. Only he who is foolish enough to lose his life finds it. It's the grain of wheat which falls into the ground and *dies* that lives.

But Jesus didn't tell his followers to love their enemies because love would or would not work. The idea probably never occurred to him to raise the question of whether or not it was practical. He told them that they should do it "that they might be sons of their spiritual Father." It was quite evident from the sunshine and rain that the Father didn't limit his love to those who loved him and obeyed him, and it was to be expected that the son should partake of the Father's nature. This course of conduct would flow as naturally from them as it would from him. Being what he is, God can't help loving all men, regardless of what they are. Even so with God's sons. Their nature is not determined by the reaction of their enemies, but by their relationship to the Father. So in a way, Christians are at the complete mercy of their enemies, since by virtue of their complete surrender to the divine will they no longer have the freedom to cease being what they are. Bound by this higher loyalty, the argument of practicality is irrelevant to them. They do not for the sake of convenience set aside their nature, any more than a minnow transforms itself into a bird when in danger of being swallowed by a bass.

Of course, one does not *have* to be a son of God. It is purely a voluntary matter, though the choice is the difference between life and death. Yet if one does choose to become a son, then one of the conditions is that you "love the outsiders and pray for those who try to do you in." Hate is a denial of sonship, because the Father, not having it in his own nature, never transmits it to his offspring. Or if one confines his love to his own circle, he identifies himself not with God, who loves universally, but with the racketeers and pagans, who limit their love to those who love them.

So Jesus lays upon kingdom citizens the obligation to be "mature, as your heavenly Father is mature." There has been much misunderstanding of this verse because of the translation "perfect" and because the verse is usually considered apart from its context. The Greek word translated "perfect" means to be perfected, or completed, or finished. It means to have all the parts, to have reached full maturity or the desired end. It is the word Jesus used on the cross when he cried, "It is finished." He didn't mean, "This is perfect," but that this was the completion of that phase of his ministry. It had come to its desired end. Paul also uses the word in 1 Corinthians 13:9-10. "For we know by parts and we prophesy by parts, but when that which is complete comes it supersedes that which is partial." Love, being whole, takes precedence over knowledge and prophecy, which are incomplete. Paul likens it to reaching maturity. Love is the adult stage. Without it, people "talk like a baby, think like a baby, act like a baby." Love is that which makes a man "outgrow childish things" and become mature.

This is almost exactly what Jesus means when he says, "Now you, you all must be mature, as your spir-

itual Father is mature." To talk about unlimited retaliation is babyish; to speak of limited retaliation is
childish; to advocate limited love is adolescent; to practice unlimited love is evidence of maturity. It is the
Father's desire that his sons become adults like himself.

To be perfect, then, really means to quit acting like
a child and to grow up. Is this an impossible command
or an unreasonable request for Jesus to make of his
followers?

But like the Jew of old who sought a definition of
"neighbor" (Luke 10:29), some Christians have been
seeking to justify themselves with the question, "And
who is my enemy?" An effort is made to classify enemies
as personal or national, vicious or gentle, sane or insane,
hopeless or redeemable. Unfortunately (or perhaps for-
tunately), Jesus never answered the qustion. If he had,
he might have told a story like the parable of the "Good
Samaritan," except that we perhaps would have called
it the "Mean Priest" or the "Horrible Levite."

Nor did Jesus explain just what he meant by love.
And Christians are still wondering about it. They
wonder if fighting might sometimes be an expression of
love, if perhaps certain conditions must be set up prior
to exercising love, if there's a personal responsibility
when executing a state's orders.

We just don't know all the answers. Even if we did,
we couldn't be sure we had all the questions.

Until we know better, a safe guide for the Christian
is to love all people. And a good definition of love is
that given by Paul in the thirteenth chapter of First
Corinthians:

"Love is long-suffering and kind. Love is not envious,
nor does it strut and brag. It does not act up, nor try

to get things for itself. It pitches no tantrums, keeps no books on insults or injuries, sees no fun in wickedness, but rejoices when truth prevails. Love is all-embracing, all-trusting, all-hoping, all-enduring. Love never quits" (1 Corinthians 13:4-7, *Cotton Patch Version*).

Without this love, Paul says it's like looking at your brother through a trick mirror ("through a glass, darkly"). He appears distorted and misshapen and maybe inhuman. But with this love, you see him face to face as he really is. Your knowledge of him is no longer in part, but full. You'll understand him as the Father and the fellowship understand you.

# 8 Testing Our Motives, Part 1

"Take heed that ye do not your righteousness before men, to be seen of them: else ye have no reward with your Father who is in heaven" (Matthew 6:1).

"But when thou doest alms, let not thy left hand know what thy right hand doeth: that thine alms may be in secret: and thy Father who seeth in secret shall recompense thee" (Matthew 6:3-4).

"Moreover when ye fast, be not, as the hypocrites, of a sad countenance: for they disfigure their faces, that they may be seen of men to fast. Verily I say unto you, they have received their reward" (Matthew 6:16).

*Read Matthew* 6:1-4, 16-18.

Action is absolutely essential to the building of strong character, but action without the proper motive can be positively detrimental. This is particularly true if the deeds are good and the motives are bad, because pretense and hypocrisy are the most devastating of all enemies to a healthy personality.

In the first part of the Sermon on the Mount, Jesus placed much emphasis upon action in order to show how the kingdom standards of righteousness far exceeded that of the scribes and Pharisees. He urged his disciples to go and be reconciled, to pluck out infected eyes, to turn the other cheek, to give the shirt off one's back, to go the second mile, to give without question, to lend without hesitation, to love one's enemies, to bless one's persecutors — to take strong, positive action.

But he wisely saw that men might even adopt his standard of righteousness from the wrong motives. Men could change their ways, if they thought it was the popular thing to do, without changing their reasons. To warn against this he said, "See to it that your effort to do right is not based on a desire to be popular. If it is, you'll get no help from your spiritual Father" (Matthew 6:1, *Cotton Patch Version*). "To do right" means in this case to live the Christian life, and covers every area of action. So no matter what you do as a Christian, the motive must be to please the Father.

In this connection, two things should be noticed. First, Jesus did not say that you should do *nothing* in front of men. You will recall that he already had told his disciples that they were the light of the world and they must shine *before men* in such a way that men might see them and glorify the Father. It would seem from this that he wanted them to do *everything* out in the open. To say the least, he assumed that for the most part our righteousness would be "before men," whether we liked it or not. Neither deeds nor motives can be kept secret very long, for the faintest subconscious whisperings are amplified by the personality and are broadcast to all men. "For nothing is concealed that won't be revealed, and nothing secret that won't be found out. What you say in the dark will be heard in the light, and what you whisper in somebody's ear behind closed doors, will be broadcast from the rooftops" (Luke 12:2-3, *Cotton Patch Version*). Since you can't hide your inner thoughts from men, there's little use trying to hide something as obvious as deeds.

In the second place, it should be noted that while all of our righteousness will be before men, the purpose of it should not be to win men's applause. The plaudits of men build up the ego and make it more difficult for us to dethrone self. We do our righteous deeds for the Father, who seeks the common good of all his children, rather than the exaltation of any one of them. To illustrate what he means, Jesus cites three examples which cover the whole range of man's activity. The first is almsgiving, or our dealings with others; the second is prayer, or our dealings with God; and the third is fasting, or our dealings with ourselves. In this chapter we shall discuss the first and third, reserving the study of prayer for the next chapter.

Jesus said: "For instance, when you make a gift to charity, don't make a lot of noise about it, like the phonies do at church and at civic clubs, so as to be praised by their cronies. The truth is, such praise is all they'll get out of it" (Matthew 6:2, *Cotton Patch Version*). Concerning this verse, E. M. Ligon, in *The Psychology of Christian Personality*, says:

> It was customary for a Jew who wanted an unusual portion of God's blessing or forgiveness for some sin, to do penance in the form of almsgiving. One of the customary ways was to buy a skin of water and give it to the poor. Water was scarce in Palestine, and usually obtainable only from a water-carrier. Then the carrier would stand in the street with the giver beside him and sound a trumpet and shout, "O thirsty, come for drink offering." The poor who accepted this charity paid for it by good wishes to the giver, such as, "God forgive thy sins, O giver of drink." In this way the giver obtained considerable free advertising, and supposedly some forgiveness. This sounds strangely like some of our modern givers who love "to be seen of men" to give, and who bask in the sunshine of public approval.

In rebuking the hypocrites, or play actors, for their love of the limelight, Jesus was not implying that kingdom citizens should disregard all human reactions. Public opinion is frequently a very good thing and is always a powerful thing. It helps to preserve order. Sometimes it is an expression of knowledge which the human race has gained by long and bitter experience. It plays an important role in character building, for it affords both stimulus and rebuke. It is not, therefore, to be considered lightly. Especially is it important for the Christian to be sensitive to the feelings of the brotherhood toward him.

Besides, there are times when public opinion can and should be influenced by Christian action. One courageous deed might inspire many others. Kindness, love, faith, sympathy, and generosity have a marvelous way of reproducing themselves in the hearts of others. Because of this, the Christian will not try to keep secret his good deeds which show that he himself believes in Christ's way and has taken his stand for him. He will boldly and openly live for Christ, gladly letting all men see his good works so that they might glorify the Father. He will be aware that Christ never commended secret discipleship.

Yet the kingdom citizen must forever be on his guard lest his virtue become his doom. He is light, and he must shine — but he must be absolutely impervious to praise. He knows the power of applause to make men drunk, to rob them of their self-respect, to make them whimpering, blubbering idiots groveling before the shrine of publicity, to make them use their very souls as coins to operate the jukebox that will sing their praises. For it is easy indeed to join the ranks of those for whom the sweetest music is the sound of their own name on the lips of men and the most beautiful sight is their photograph in the newspapers. It is against this sunken debauchery of the soul that Jesus warns his followers. And even though we today have dressed it up and called it by the more respectable title of "honor" and have organized societies for its perpetuation, the warning remains. Its effect upon the soul has never changed. (For a dramatic presentation of this warning, read Luke 14:7-15.)

The attitude which Jesus wants his followers to have in their dealings with others is given in a striking figure of speech. He said, "But you, when you give to charity, don't pat yourself on the back, so that your gift might be truly secret. And your Father, who sees secrets, will respond to you" (Matthew 6:3-4, *Cotton Patch Version*). The phrase "truly secret" is about the equivalent of our expression "from the heart." When one gives grudgingly or for show, his heart is not in his gift. He will reach into his pocket with his right hand, and then with his left hand he will carefully count out the exact amount he wishes to give. This enables him to keep an accurate account of his righteousness. Every deed is recorded in detail, and due pride taken therein. But when one gives in secret, or "from the heart," he reaches into his pocket with his right hand and takes out all that's there and hands it over to meet the need. He doesn't count it out; that is, his left hand never enters into the transaction. He isn't interested in *figures;* he's interested in *people*. He wants no record, any more than a mother wants a record of how many times she has warmed the baby's bottle. His is an expression of love, and love never keeps books, for it never thinks in terms of profit or loss. Stingy people always let their left hand know what their right hand is doing. They "give till it hurts," and they always know exactly how badly they are hurt. But loving, generous kingdom citizens need but one hand with which to make their gifts. They give until it's gone. Like the Father who sends sunshine and rain upon the good and bad alike, their dealings with others are based on their own inherent goodness rather than on the worthiness or unworthiness of the objects of their charity. And the Father rewards them by making them even more bighearted, just as the reward of selfishness is an increasingly selfish, stingy nature.

It is impossible, however, to be honest and sincere and without pretense in our dealings with others without tapping the inner sources of power which involve prayer and fasting. So important is prayer that all of the next chapter will be devoted to a discussion of it. But fasting is important, too, though we moderns hardly understand what is meant by it. Jesus said, "Now when you fast, don't be like the sad-eyed hypocrites, for they mark up their faces to give the appearance of fasting. I'm telling you, they have received all that's coming to them. But you, when you fast, comb your hair and wash your face so that you won't appear to be fasting toward men but toward your Father who is in the secret, and your Father who sees in the secret will reward you" (Matthew 6:16-18).

Note that Jesus did not say *"if* you fast" but *"when* you fast," apparently assuming that his disciples would. In fact, *all* men fast at one time or another, even though they may not be conscious of it. Of course some persons think they're fasting when they do without an ice cream cone on New Year's Day or when they cut out jellied veal on Sunday night or give up this or that at some season of the year. All that is but rubbish from the junkyard of the Pharisees and is clearly rebuked by the Master. It is the food that "sad-eyed hypocrites" thrive on, but it will thoroughly nauseate an honest, sincere kingdom citizen.

Jesus and his disciples avoided every appearance of the "sad-eyed, hypocritical fasting." For this reason people accused them of not being religious. On one occasion even John the Baptist's disciples found fault with Jesus on this score. They asked, "Why is it that we and the Pharisees are fasting and your disciples are not?" (Matthew 9:14). They didn't seem to understand how Jesus could be religious and not look the part. He had no clerical garb or ministerial tone to enhance his professional dignity, nor did his followers wear "religious" clothes or in any other outward way give the appearance of piety. They didn't call each other "Reverend" and "Doctor" (Matthew 23:8-10). They had no lapel buttons and no slogans. They had no fast days, and by looking at them you never would know if and when they spent all night in prayer. They simply did not look at all as religious people should have looked.

Yet Jesus said, "When you fast, comb your hair and wash your face." Obviously, fasting meant to Jesus something radically different from what it did to the Pharisees. To them it had become the brand of religiosity. But Jesus took it back to its original and deeper meaning. At first, it did not at all mean doing without food or becoming unkempt in personal appearance. It was a spontaneous expression of a deep emotional feeling and was usually associated with extreme grief. When one's heart was in great anguish, there was little desire for food, so not eating came to be associated with a deep inner experience. Especially when men were deeply grieved over their sins and were desperately seeking God's forgiveness, they paid little attention to such material things as food and clothing. Finally, the external evidences of fasting became mistaken for the real experience.

So fasting really means to "move fast" toward a dominating objective. If taking time to prepare food, or shave, or have your trousers pressed slows you down and prevents you from "fasting" toward your objective, you will do without those things. For instance, a man might be "fasting" toward money, that is, his one consuming desire is to "make it," so he will frequently be "too busy to eat." Or one might be fasting toward knowledge and not have time to sleep. The abstinence from food and sleep enables one to move faster toward his objective. When the objective is particularly desirable or popular, and men want to give the impression that they are pursuing it so as to win the praise and admiration of their fellowmen, they will fake the evidences of fasting. This is particularly true of men wanting to appear religious without really wanting God.

To some extent, then, all men fast, in that at some time or another there comes into their lives a deep concern or obsession that is stronger than bread and meat. It may be long-lived or short-lived, but as long as it is there men will "fast." The trouble is that too many men get their signals mixed and their sense of values distorted and they move in the wrong direction — toward money or fame or pleasure or profession. They move fast — toward destruction. Also, there are always those spiritual mimics who wear the heavenly robes while riding the highway to hell.

Though Jesus had more patience with the honest fasters, even though they were going in the wrong direction, than he had with the hypocrites, his desire was that men fast "toward the Father." That's the way he did it. A good example was when he had been pouring out his heart to the sinful Samaritan woman at the well and had forgotten all about food. When his disciples returned with some and said, "Rabbi, eat," he said, "I have food to eat that you don't know about." When they began asking each other if someone had given him something to eat, he said, "My food is to do the will of him who sent me and to finish his task" (John 4:31-34). He was so absorbed in accomplishing the task of the Father that to have stopped for physical bread would have slowed him down; that is, it would have prevented him from "fasting."

Kingdom citizens fast, not when they do so outwardly by abstaining from food or wearing certain kinds of clothing or going through ceremonial forms, but when the spirit of Jesus Christ dwells in them in such a compelling way that his kingdom is their chief concern. Nothing comes above it — neither food nor job nor friends nor family; neither pleasure nor clothes nor fame nor honor. Absolute loyalty to Jesus and his kingdom is the Christian's fast.

# 9 Testing Our Motives, Part 2

"And when ye pray, ye shall not be as the hypocrites: for they love to stand and pray in the synagogues and in the corners of the streets, that they may be seen of men. Verily I say unto you, They have received their reward. But thou, when thou prayest, enter into thine inner chamber, and having shut thy door, pray to thy Father who is in secret, and thy Father who seeth in secret shall recompense thee. And in praying use not vain repetitions, as the Gentiles do: for they think that they shall be heard for their much speaking" (Matthew 6:5-7).
*Read Matthew 6:5-15.*

Absolute sincerity is the mark of the true Christian. His righteousness exceeds the righteousness of the scribes and Pharisees in that he is honest in his dealings —with others, with self, and with God. Already we have examined what Jesus taught in the Sermon on the Christian's dealings with self and others. In this chapter we shall examine his relation to God, particularly in the area of prayer.

What Jesus said is very plain. "And when you pray, don't be like the phonies. For they love to stand up and pray in church and at public occasions, so they might build a reputation as pray-ers. The truth is, that's all they'll get out of it. But you, when you pray, go to your bedroom, shut the door and pray to your Father in private. And your seeing Father will privately participate with you" (Matthew 6:5-6, *Cotton Patch Version*).

The nature of the phony and that of the sincere Christian are vividly contrasted here as each prepares for prayer. The hypocrite, whose motive is to impress men and receive their applause, selects his place of prayer with those things in mind. He chooses what would today be the main auditorium of the church at the eleven o'clock worship service. Nor does he assume the customary prone position of a Jew at prayer, for that would make him too inconspicuous. He must stand. In order to impress further people with his piety, and for the benefit of those who did not go to church, the phony makes additional prayers during the week at various public occasions and in public places. Though his prayers probably aren't heard — he doesn't intend for them to be — he does get himself seen and rewarded, with either a curse or a blessing. At least he's in the public eye.

Having a different spirit, the Christian naturally makes different preparations. His object in praying is fellowship with the Father and power from on high. It would do no good for men to hear his prayer, for men can't answer it. They do not have that for which he seeks. Only the Father can reward him. Consequently, he does his praying privately, alone, with the Father.

You may feel that you cannot follow Jesus' teaching here, for you have no private place of prayer. "I don't have a private room," you say. Neither did Jesus; he didn't even have a bedroom (Matthew 8:20). But you can be alone with the Father even with other people around you. Your heart can signal quiet messages of prayer to the Father even while you ride a bus, while you are at work, while you are in school.

And you can sometimes find those private places Jesus

found — a wilderness (Luke 4:42), a mountaintop (Matthew 14:23), and a garden (John 18:1). No job, no city wall, no busy engagements kept Jesus away from these private places of prayer.

Does Jesus' insistence upon privacy in prayer mean that we should have no public prayers? No, for we know that the early church prayed as a group (Acts 1:24-25; 12:5). It is not praying in public that Jesus condemned, but praying "to be seen of men." We cannot help wondering, however, how many public prayers there would really be today if we should eliminate those intended primarily for the ears of men.

Jesus felt, too, that prayers could be greatly shortened. "And while you are praying," he said, "don't jabber like pagans, who think that their long-windedness will get them an answer. Don't you be like them, for your Father knows what you need before you ever ask him" (Matthew 6:7-8, *Cotton Patch Version*). To the pagans, God was a celestial landlord who had to be worried into fixing things up for them. They made sure that God was informed (in high-sounding, dignified language, of course) of the terrible mess that his earthly estate was in and how badly that part of it in which they lived needed patching up. They had either too much rain or too little; it was either too hot or too cold; their rent was too high, their income too low; their job was good, but the boss was bad; profits were wonderful, but labor was terrible; things were getting scarce, and a war was coming on. For goodness' sake, couldn't God do something about this creation of his?

On the other hand, the kingdom citizen was not on a landlord-tenant arrangement; it was a Father-son relationship. He quietly trusted the Father to anticipate and supply all his physical needs while he devoted himself completely to the accomplishing of the Father's work on earth. Much of his praying was listening and giving of himself and his will to God. His desire was not to use God but to be used by him. These were the things in his heart, but he needed the Master to teach him how to say them.

So Jesus said: "So here's the way you all should pray:

'Father of us, O Spiritual One,
Your Name be truly honored.
Your kingdom spread, your will prevail
Through earth, as through the heavens.
Sustaining bread grant us each day.
Forgive our debts as we forgive
The debts of all who cannot pay.
And from confusion keep us clear;
Deliver us from evil's sway.' "
(Matthew 6:9-13, *Cotton Patch Version*)

Fifty-three simple words (fifty-seven in the Greek), yet their influence on the world has been immeasurable! This prayer has been upon the lips of more men than any other bit of the world's greatest literature. No doubt Jesus himself lavished great thought upon it, for in the Greek it is in the form of a poem, having definite rhyme and meter. In every respect it is a spiritual gem, polished, and brought to high luster by the Master himself. It is not the "Lord's Prayer," but our prayer which the Lord gave us. Let us examine it carefully in order to understand it more clearly.

"Father," it begins. This is the bravest, most dazzling word that Jesus could have put upon human lips. We have become so accustomed to it that we are not aware of the tremendous impact it must have had upon Jesus' original hearers. They were those who had been taught to stand in holy awe of the Most High. So greatly was he feared that they dared not even to use his name. Job's conception of him was very prevalent. God spoke from a whirlwind, in words like these: "Who is this that darkeneth counsel by words without knowledge? Where wast thou when I laid the foundations of the earth? Declare, if thou hast understanding. Who determined the measures thereof, if thou knowest? Or who stretched the line upon it? Whereupon were the foundations thereof fastened? Or who laid the cornerstone thereof, when the morning stars sang together?" (Job 38:2-6). And Job's response to him was very typical. "Behold, I am of small account; what shall I answer thee? I lay my hand upon my mouth. . . . I had heard of thee by the hearing of the ear; but now mine eye seeth thee. Wherefore, I abhor myself, and repent in dust and ashes" (Job 40:4; 42:5-6).

Only once in all the Old Testament did a prophet dare to burst forth with the idea that God might be a Father. Isaiah sings, "Unto us a son is given; and the government shall be upon his shoulder: and his name shall be called Wonderful, Counselor, Mighty God, Everlasting Father, Prince of Peace" (Isaiah 9:6). But even this is not a direct reference to God, but to his Messiah. There simply was nothing like it in Judaism before Jesus boldly taught men to say "Father."

This conception of God has two great implications. First, it assures us that the universe is fatherly and friendly. It is not hostile. Men are not weevils caught in the grinding burrs of the corn mill. The world of the spirit is not a world of spooks and hobgoblins and witches. He who sits in the heavens is our Friend and is kind; he is our Father and is loving. Because Jesus knew this to be so, he quieted men's anxieties more than once with his gentle "Be not afraid therefore." This truth was the clue, then, as it is today, to a life without fear. In it is the key to mental and spiritual as well as physical health.

The second thing which this concept of God does is to elevate the human soul to the plane of the divine. When the believer calls God "Father," he implies that he himself is a son. Being a son, he is of infinite value to the Father and his brothers. He is worth saving and being forgiven — and he is loved. He is expected to walk worthily of his high calling. This knowledge of his worth and this divine expectation of the best from him lifts him to unexcelled heights of power and joy. So, in that one word is enough to dispel all our fears, to forgive all our sins, and to make available an unlimited source of power.

"Father of *us*," goes the prayer. What is meant by "us"? Does it include everybody — *all* men? It is obvious that Jesus did not think so. He drew a clear line between kingdom citizens and "pagans," and warned his followers not to be like the latter, particularly in their prayer life. Then he gave this prayer *to his disciples* and told *them* to pray in this manner. Now it is true that God is the Father of all men in the sense that he created them, but in the spiritual sense he is the Father of believers only. And this is the way Jesus meant it, for he said, "Father of us, O Spiritual One." Consequently, not all men are brothers, except in a physical sense due to their common fleshly ancestry, though one would hardly use the word "brothers" to describe such a kinship. "Very distant cousins" would be more appropriate. Only the *believers* are brothers. But *all* believers are sons of the Father and brothers of one another, regardless of their race, nationality, education, money, or any other difference. And it is high time that the followers of Jesus Christ either faced up to this truth or quit repeating this prayer. For our Lord was sharper in his rebuke of the hypocrisy of the Pharisees than of the "vain repetitions" of the pagans.

Perhaps that is why he added immediately, "Your Name be truly honored." He knew the awful tendency of the human heart toward hypocrisy. He knew that men could call God "Father," proclaiming themselves as his sons, and take the Father's name (as being in his family) and then keep right on living as sons of the Devil. They take God's name, but they take it in vain. They are play actors, hypocrites, using the Father's holy name as a mask to cover their shameful iniquity. Jesus wanted no such people among his followers. Citizens of his kingdom — *"Christ-ians"* — were given a new name, and he intended that they should take it seriously and sincerely, and keep it ever sacred and holy.

For it is only the sincere who can continue the prayer: "Your kingdom spread — your will prevail — Through earth, as through the heavens." A true citizen passionately longs for his country's success. He believes in it and wants to see it grow and spread. He zealously advocates its ideals and rejoices when men accept them. And so it is with the kingdom citizen. He knows that his citizenship is in heaven, but he is not content that it should remain in storage there. He wants others to share in it, to come into the fellowship, to be a son of God in the Father's family. Though his citizenship in the kingdom is to him the pearl of great price, a treasure hid in the field, it never becomes a gem to be hoarded but rather it is yeast to be multiplied and salt to be shared. He would not sell it for anything, nor dare to keep it for anything. He is eternally restless until Christ's kingdom comes upon earth — the whole earth.

The kingdom's coming is more than just a spiritual thing, though the spirit is certainly its fountainhead. The sense of this verse seems to imply this: As the kingdom of God and his will become increasingly real to us in the spirit, it should be taken out of the realm of theory and translated into the earthly relationships of life. "Through earth [physically], as through the heavens [spiritually]." In other words, we should pray that the spiritual and physical development of the kingdom should keep pace with each other.

When we pray that the kingdom might become a present reality upon the earth, it is assumed that we will give ourselves as diligent workers in this mighty undertaking. Lest we faint, we shall need nourishment. But the Father has already anticipated our needs and has made out a wholesome menu. In gratitude we turn to him with the simple cry, "Sustaining bread grant us each day." This is an expression of complete trust in the Father to supply all the needs, both spiritual and physical, of those who seek first his kingdom on earth.

But one cannot be an efficient worker in bringing others into the kingdom if there is aught between him and others, whether they be in the fellowship or out of it. He must "forgive men their offenses," for this is the condition upon which the Father grants his forgiveness.

One meets the Father on one's way *back* from being reconciled with his brother.

The petition, "from confusion keep us clear; Deliver us from evil's sway," poses a problem. Does this mean that God does sometimes cause man to be confused, or does it mean that God tests man, or what? It may be that this verse was not a part of the original prayer of Jesus. The chain of thought, so some say, is more natural and logical if we omit verse thirteen entirely. But the first part of the verse does occur also in Luke. We know certainly that God does not tempt man in an evil sense. On the other hand, God does allow man to be tested. For instance, we read in the Old Testament that God proved Abraham (Genesis 22:1); that is, God put Abraham to the test. The familiar story of Job also shows how God permitted his servant Job to go through many trials, but he would not allow Satan to touch Job's soul, and through all the struggle Job remained true to God. Even Jesus met the Tempter on the Mount of Temptation, and there were the dark hours upon the cross. But Jesus won the victory.

Is it not therefore logical that this prayer should contain a petition which recognizes man's struggle with sin, and the absolute necessity of having God's power if he is to overcome the evil one?

If we lack a reverent, vital, living expression of this prayer, our lives will suffer. In it is the secret to great power. But it is not released by vain repetition. Pagans, even though they call themselves by Christ's name, never taste its essence. For this is the prayer of the totally committed, the wholly surrendered, the completely dedicated citizens of the kingdom of God.

# 10 The Measure of a Treasure

"Lay not up for yourselves treasures upon the earth, where moth and rust consume, and where thieves break through and steal; but lay up for yourselves treasures in heaven, where neither moth nor rust doth consume, and where thieves do not break through nor steal: for where thy treasure is, there will thy heart be also" (Matthew 6:19-21).

"But seek ye first his kingdom, and his righteousness; and all these things shall be added unto you" (Matthew 6:33).

*Read Matthew* 6:19-34.

Why is a new mail-order catalog so fascinating to millions of people? Is it the pictures? Or the new fashions and gadgets? Partly, but the book would be dull indeed were it not for the *prices.* By carefully studying it, one can get a good idea of the relative value of the things advertised. And this greatly aids one in making a wise, efficient use of his money.

All of life is something of a mail-order catalog, and a wise man is he who studies it and knows the relative value of things. He has learned to take the measure of a treasure. He can value values. He knows what belongs first in life.

But a man wise in one area might be a fool in another. He might know the worth of stocks and bonds and not know the value of his own soul.

It is not strange that "worship" is a contraction of

"worth-ship." For religion has always been a key factor in aiding one to evaluate *all* of life properly. Jesus was particularly careful to give his disciples detailed instructions along this line. He said, "Don't all of you value for yourselves material values, which worms and rust ultimately consume and which thieves break into and steal. But you value for yourselves spiritual values, which neither worms nor rust consume and which thieves do not break into and steal. For what you value is what you shall be."

There are two measuring rods with which a treasure may be measured. One is the rod of the world, or the material mind. Its readings are in "rings and things" — money, power, prestige, clothes, houses, lands, pleasure — and misery, though this is usually a big figure written in tiny letters. This gauge is constructed on the principle that a man's life consists in the abundance of his possessions. With this stick the world generally measures "success." Countless thousands of young people "choose a vocation" on the basis of its readings. For men of business and finance, it is Aaron's rod. For all men, rich and poor alike, who do not have the mind of Christ, its glittering figures have an unusual attraction.

And here is a great mystery: Why has the Western world, and America in particular, which measures most of its values on this materialistic scale, been attracted to the religion of Jesus Christ inasmuch as Jesus ruthlessly condemns materialism? What trick of the mind has made it possible for us and him to dwell together in apparent unity?

Certainly he has given to us another rod — the mind of the spirit. It is the length and breadth and height of Christ's own life. By it — rather, by him — the Christian measures all things.

When the two rods are placed side by side, behold, they are exact opposites. The first on one is the last on the other, and the last on one is the first on the other. On the material gauge, things like love, humility, unselfishness, and honesty appear as trifles, while a big salary and a slick automobile get a high rating. On the spiritual gauge, this is reversed.

If you decide to follow Jesus, you will value spiritual values. You will set your mind on the things which are above, where Christ is. You will have in you the mind which was in Christ Jesus. And this mind will be able to discern clearly that material things, be they ever so attractive, are but worm food, rust, and objects of thievery, when viewed in the light of eternity. You will see that a man's life consists not in the abundance of things which he possesses.

But must we choose between these two? Can't we get our scale of values first from one and then the other? Isn't there some good in both of them? Let Jesus answer.

"The body depends on the eyes for light. Now if your eyes are in focus, then the body will have clear light. But if your eyes are not in focus, then your whole body will be in confused darkness" (Matthew 6:22-23, *Cotton Patch Version*).

Your sense of values is to the soul what the eye is to the body. It enables you to see things in their proper perspective. It enables you to get your bearings and a sense of direction. But the eye must be in focus. If both eyes are fastened on a single objective, then you are seeing clearly — you are not confused. But if your eye is out of focus from attempting to look at more than one object at a time, your "light" will be darkness; you will see nothing clearly.

So Jesus is saying that to try to regulate your life by both standards of measurement is like a man who tries to look at two things at once and sees neither. You will be utterly confused. You must focus your life upon one way or the other. You must choose whether you are going to look upon things through the eyes of Christ or the eyes of the world.

Jesus expresses the same thought again in different words. He says, "Nobody can be a slave to two masters, for either he will hate the one and love the other, or he will be loyal to the one and disloyal to the other. You can't be a slave to God and Mammon" (v. 24). Notice that he doesn't say that you *shouldn't* serve two masters, but that you *can't*. This is not advice — it is law, as inexorable as the law of gravity. It's like stating that you can't follow a road that forks. It is based on the assumption that the mind of God and the mind of the secular world are in direct contradiction to each other. They give two conflicting standards of measurement. Loyalty must be given to one or the other.

It won't work, either, to hire out to Mammon and give a tenth of your wages to God. Not even if you raise his cut to a fifth, or a half.

Nor do you have to deal in big figures to be Mammon's slave. All you need is a materialistic set of values. But don't think that getting out of silks into blue denim automatically makes you God's slave. He wants you to change your loyalty, then your clothes. Once you have become his slave, clothes, jewelry, furs, furniture, and all such have a way of adjusting themselves. (As an illustration of how Christianity broke up a thriving jewelry business, read Acts 19:23-41.)

Because Jesus' disciples cannot be slaves to Mammon and because it is the master's responsibility to care for his slaves, the Lord continues, "Therefore I say to you, don't worry about your living, what you shall eat or what you shall drink; nor about your body, what you shall put on. Isn't your life more valuable than food and your body than clothing? Look there at the birds in the sky. They don't plant or harvest or store up in barns, and your spiritual Father nurses them. Aren't all of you more valuable than they? Now who among you, by worrying over it, can make himself one inch taller? And why worry about clothes? Consider how the lilies of the field grow. They don't scrub and sew, but I'm telling you that not even Solomon in all his finery was clad like one of them. Now if God so dresses up the wild flowers which are blooming one day and thrown into the fire the next, will he not do much more for you, O you who trust too little? So stop worrying and raising the questions, 'What will we eat?' and 'What will we drink?' and 'What will we wear?' for all these are the things that pagans go in for. Your spiritual Father knows that you need all these things. But you make the kingdom and its righteousness your chief concern, and all these things will be added to you. Therefore, don't worry over tomorrow, for tomorrow will worry over itself. One day's evil is sufficient" (vv. 25-34).

Now let's get one thing straight. This isn't a pious, mushy pat on the back, telling men not to worry any more, that if they'll let go and let God, he'll fix everything up for them slick as a whistle. A true friend of the burdened, oppressed, laboring people, as Jesus was, wouldn't feed them "pie in the sky in the sweet bye and bye." He knew how bread came, for he himself had sweated for it.

And he would want it crystal clear that these words were not addressed to disciples of Mammon. It is a grave injustice to lead Mammonites to believe that they were. These people should be frankly told to look to their own master for sustenance, for Mammon also makes certain agreements with those who seek first his kingdom. His outfit is run on the principle of profit, and as long as a slave is profitable, he will be cared for. But Mammon makes no promises to the aged, the sick, the widows, the orphans, the ignorant — in short, the profitless. So by all means, Mammon's disciples should make every possible provision, while they are healthful and profitable, for the time will come when they will be discarded. They will be fools indeed to take no thought for the morrow, to store up nothing in barns. They will need life insurance and annuities, social security, investments, savings accounts, and anything else to help them to answer the questions: "What will we eat? What will we drink? What will we wear?" Jesus freely granted that the pagans (disciples of Mammon) sought after all these things. It was an absolute necessity with them. Their system demanded it.

It is perfectly obvious that Jesus could have addressed his remarks only to those who "make the kingdom and its righteousness their chief concern." He told *his disciples* — kingdom citizens — to look at the birds *in the sky* and to consider the lilies *of the fields*. They were nourished and cared for *because they were in the environment and plan and purpose which the Father intended for them.* They must stay within that plan if they are to claim the Father's care. Suppose they had the power of free will, as man does, and the bird chose to live under water and the lily decided to live on concrete? Would the Father feed and clothe them? He might wish to, but he could not. He would be thwarted in his purposes by their wills. He can care for men *only on his terms.*

The environment which God intends for all men is the kingdom. It is the summation of all his plans and purposes. It is the framework of his will. Men in it are like birds in the sky and lilies of the field — they are living in harmony with God's design. And being of more value than either, men have a perfectly natural right to expect more from the Father's bounty. Then why *should they worry?* If the Father knows their needs, as he obviously does, and has promised to meet them, why not trust him completely?

But how does God "add all these things" to kingdom citizens? Does he rain them from the skies or provide them miraculously merely "in answer to prayer"? Certainly not. That isn't the way he does it for the birds and lilies. They are nourished *from the system to which they have committed themselves.* The needs of kingdom citizens are supplied *through the kingdom.* It is God's distributing agency.

Let's be more specific and turn to an actual illustration. In the book of Acts we are told that the Holy Spirit came upon 120 people on the day of Pentecost. This powerful, indwelling Spirit brought them, and

three thousand more shortly thereafter, into the kingdom, into the love relationship with God and their
brethren. One result of this tremendous inward change
was a radically different attitude toward possessions.
Luke was so amazed at it that he described it twice
(Acts 2:44-45; 4:32-35). He said, "Now the heart and
soul of the multitude of believers was one, and not a
one of them claimed any of his possessions for himself,
but all things were shared by them. And with great
power the apostles were exhibiting the evidence of the
Lord Jesus' resurrection, and everybody was greatly de-
lighted. *For there wasn't among them anyone in need.*
Those who were owners of lands and houses sold them
and brought the proceeds of the sale and turned them
over to the apostles." The narrative continues by citing
what must have been two typical responses. Barnabas,
entering wholeheartedly into the fellowship, sold a field
and turned in *all* the receipts. He later became a pillar
in the church. Ananias and Sapphira, in an effort to
serve God and Mammon, had a sale and brought *part*
of the money. It was the worst and last thing they ever
did. Their funeral was held the same day.

How did it happen that there wasn't a needy person
among these people? Had more food, clothing, and
shelter been miraculously created? No, but a new way
of life had been adopted. Need, not greed, became the
principle by which they lived. By partaking of the spirit
of Jesus, they became new citizens of the kingdom of
God. Sharing completely with one another in love and
unity and making distribution according to the new
standard of measurement, they took the assets *which
God had already given them* and cared for those in
need.

This is a vivid illustration of the Christian principle of love, of concern for the needs of others, and of stewardship of the possessions God lends to us. Men through all ages since Jesus lived on earth, and through differing economic systems, have been Christian. The man who makes Mammon his god drives out love and refuses to live by the principles of the kingdom.

When God first made man, he made provision for all man's needs. This has been true ever since. God has already "added all these things." There is enough in the world today to meet all men's needs. The problem is not in supply but in distribution, not with God but with man. Poverty and riches are the result of man's rebellion against the will of God. When his kingdom comes, when his will is done on earth, both poverty and riches will go!

# 11 Danger of Self-Righteous Judging

"Judge not, that ye be not judged. For with what judgment ye judge, ye shall be judged: and with what measure ye mete, it shall be measured unto you. And why beholdest thou the mote that is in thy brother's eye, but considerest not the beam that is in thine own eye? Or how wilt thou say to thy brother, Let me cast out the mote out of thine eye; and lo, the beam is in thine own eye? Thou hypocrite, cast out first the beam out of thine own eye; and then shalt thou see clearly to cast out the mote out of thy brother's eye" (Matthew 7:1-5).

The measuring rod of the kingdom is indeed a mighty thing. Nations, races, churches, and individuals are judged by it, and judgment is a serious business. It is a tremendous responsibility. The qualifications for exercising it are high.

Jesus knew that it was not enough to give to kingdom citizens a new measuring stick; he must instruct them in its use. So he says, "Don't act as a judge in order to escape being judged." Observe that he does not simply say, "Judge not." People frequently quote this verse as though Jesus forbids all forms of moral discrimination. They regard lightly or overlook completely such things as lying, cheating, stealing, or playing the hypocrite, on the grounds that one should not judge his fellow man.

Either these people are so weak of character that they

are afraid to take a stand, or they quote this verse in self-defense. A liar quite naturally does not want his lying brought to trial. A thief most certainly advocates tolerance toward his thieving. A hypocrite wants no one to adjust his mask. So in chorus they say, "Judge not!" What they really mean is "Judge *me* not." They have no objection to judgment of other people; in fact, they're usually glad to lend a hand with it.

Certainly this idea is foreign to the thought of Jesus. He took for granted that it would be necessary for kingdom citizens both to judge and be judged. He told them to learn to tell the difference between a sheepskin with a sheep in it and a sheepskin with a wolf in it. He also said that a tree should be judged by its fruit. He himself was sitting in constant judgment upon people who tithed even their spices and garden produce and overlooked the judgment and love of God (Luke 11: 42), who strutted about seeking the places of prominence in the synagogues and idle flattery in the streets, who scrupulously washed the outside of their pots and pans and left the inside filthy. In fact, he condemned the whole system of the Pharisees by telling them that they were like old, unmarked graves which people walk over without even knowing that anybody is buried there (Luke 11:44). Though they were unaware of it, the Pharisees had been dead so long that there was no longer any evidence of their graves.

How could Jesus judge men and systems so ruthlessly and then tell his disciples not to exercise the same judgment? He didn't. He knew that if they were the kind of men and women that kingdom citizens should be they would have to judge. But the thing he wanted to make clear to them was that when one assumes the role of judge he is not thereby exempt from judgment himself. In other words, don't sit on the judgment seat with the idea that you'll never be required to stand in the prisoner's box. "For you shall be judged by the sentences you pass, and you shall be measured by the measures you mete." The same standard applies to both judge and prisoner, to both preacher and congregation.

Perhaps it would help us to understand Jesus' point a bit better if we paraphrased it like this: "Don't become a preacher for the purpose of not being preached to, for with the same sermons you preach you shall be preached to, and the same conduct you prescribe for others shall be prescribed for you." Stated positively, this verse is an admonition to *practice what you preach.*

Judge we must and preach we must, but these are no substitutes for applied Christianity. Being an authority on the Scriptures doesn't release one from the exacting demands of Bible truth. Denouncing the world's sins is of no avail if you yourself partake of the same thing. Effective sermons come from the laboratory, not the classroom. Men are judged only when the Word becomes flesh and dwells among them. John puts it this way: "My little ones, let's not *talk* about love. Let's not *sing* about love. Let's put love into action and make it real" (1 John 3:18 [1 Jack], *Cotton Patch Version*).

Paul says it even more bluntly: "O teacher of another, do you teach yourself? O preacher against stealing, do you steal? O opponent of adultery, do you commit adultery? O hater of idols, do you plunder their shrines?" (Romans 2:21-22). Paul is not saying that there should be no condemnation of these things, but that setting oneself up as a teacher and preacher against them constitutes no excuse for indulging in them. One is not exempt from the laws of health by becoming a doctor, nor the laws of the mind by becoming a psychologist, nor the laws of the spirit by becoming a church member.

So it is not judging, but *self-righteous judging*, against which Jesus warns his disciples. Honest, sincere judging is good, but hypocritical judging is perilous. Nothing will destroy a fellowship more quickly than to have within it a brother who carries around with him a folding judgment-seat which makes it possible for him to pass judgment on another brother anywhere, any time. His tongue is usually loose on both ends with ball bearings in the middle. He goes on the theory that he makes himself bigger by making someone else smaller. He has a high regard for his ability to analyze men and motives and is utterly incensed if one seeks to reverse his judicial opinions.

But, as always, his judgments reveal his true nature, for a man's opinions of his neighbors are an eternally reliable index of his own character. At no time does his real self become more evident than when he is sitting on his folding judgment-seat giving his opinions of others. A liar will invariably conclude that most men are like himself — liars; it is the opinion of a thief that they are thieves; while an honest man is quite certain that others are honest.

The story goes that a man wishing to find a place to settle drove into a rural community and inquired of an old farmer what kind of people lived there. In reply, the farmer asked, "Stranger, what kind of people live in the community you came from?" "They are bad people," he said. "Gossips, slanderers, cheapskates." The old man shook his head. "You might as well move on," he said, "because that's the kind of people who live here, too."

Later on, another man came through seeking a place to live, and he asked the same old farmer about the people. "How were the people where you came from?" inquired the farmer. "Wonderful, simply wonderful," he said. "They were thoughtful, kind, loving. I surely hated to leave them." "Unload," beamed the farmer, "because that's the kind of people you'll find around here."

Not only may others size up a person by the judgment with which he judges others, but a man's condemnation of others becomes his own most severe punishment. For instance, here is a person who is a slanderous gossip. His conclusion is that since he gossips, all men gossip. So when he sees several of his acquaintances together, he is quite sure that they are doing what he would be doing—gossiping. His guilt and inflated ego combine to make him believe they are gossiping *about him,* even though they may really be talking about the weather. He has had this feeling so frequently that he is raw and extremely sensitive and touchy about it. Consequently, nothing is capable of inflicting more torture upon him than gossip—about him. Whether the gossip is real or imaginary is of no consequence; the punishment is the same.

By this same process, one who lies reacts most violently when he is lied to; one who deceives, when he is deceived; one who is dishonest, when he is treated dishonestly; one who hates, when he is hated. The opposite is also true. No one reacts more tenderly to love than one who loves; to kindness than one who is kind; to humility than one who is humble; to forgiveness than one who forgives. It's just the plain truth that "with what judgment you judge you shall be judged." You determine your own punishment or reward. You reap *what* you sow. Paul also puts it this way: "Now listen here, man — and that includes every preacher — you have nothing to hide behind. For whenever you preach to somebody else, you're laying it on yourself, because you, the preacher, are guilty of the very same things" (Romans 2:1, *Cotton Patch Version*).

The faults in others which offend you most are in all probability your own faults coming home to roost. And you either have to put up with their squawking or get rid of the birds.

That's no doubt what Jesus was driving at when he said, "Why examine the splinter in your brother's eye, and take no notice of the plank in your own eye? Or how can you say to your brother, 'Bud, hold still while I pick that splinter out of your eye,' when there is a plank in yours? Listen, you phony, first pull the plank from your eye and then you'll be able to see better to get the splinter out of your brother's eye" (Matthew 7:3-5, *Cotton Patch Version*).

It is a bad thing to have even a tiny speck in the eye, to say nothing of a splinter. By all means it should be removed quickly. If the person can't do it himself, he should have help.

Though it is an extremely delicate operation, the first to volunteer his services is old Plank-Eye himself who gropes his way toward you. He has known all along that you had the splinter (natural for him, of course, because it probably came off his plank), but he just hasn't been quite sure how to approach you about it. Of course, you know he's an expert splinter-picker — he has been at it all his life. He doesn't want to hurt you either. No hard feelings or anything like that, understand. He really hates to be so frank, but since it's for your own good — wham! He bumps into you so hard that with the plank protruding from his eye, he well-nigh puts out *both* your eyes! Your bleeding face and blinding pain cause him to believe that the operation is successfully over. Plank-Eye feels warm inside because he has been able to render such incalculable service.

But the kingdom citizen has little in common with Plank-Eye. He knows that on occasions it is imperative that the splinter be removed from the eye of a brother, but before engaging in this difficult task he cleanses his own soul more thoroughly than any doctor scours his hands prior to a delicate operation. He feels the tremendous responsibility of judging and is aware of the danger of causing serious or permanent injury. It is only when one approaches his brother with clean hands and pure heart and clear eyes that he is qualified to deal with his brother's faults. But usually when one clears up his own attitude and puts his own house in order, he finds that his brother's faults have pretty well disappeared. Frequently another's "splinter" is merely a reflection in that person's eyes of the beam in one's own eyes.

It should be again emphasized that it is primarily for the welfare of kingdom citizens that Jesus warns them against censorious judging. For the one who judges harshly is the one who is most hurt by it. Similarly, hate hurts the hater more than the hated; or jealousy, or greed, or pride blight the personalities of those who harbor them. These things are death-dealing germs which prey upon the mind and soul. Even small amounts of them can cause serious illness.

And they are very contagious. Yet it is well-nigh impossible to quarantine those people who are afflicted with them. So be careful that you neither carry nor contract the disease. Be eternally on your guard. Especially keep the tongue well bridled. Form your acquaintances among those who do likewise. Unless you are a very, very mature Christian, compliment a brother's virtues but refrain altogether from dealing with his vices. In the rare cases when they must be dealt with, do it to his face, in private, in a cool atmosphere which has been sterilized against anger, tension, and pride. Obviously, you will need the spirit and presence of the Master.

It is possible that Jesus was still talking about self-righteous judging when he said,

"Don't throw your valuables to the dogs,
And don't spread your pearls before the hogs;
Or they will trample them under their feet
And even turn and bite you" (Matthew 7:6, *Cotton Patch Version*).

Some say that this verse means that we should not present Christian truth to people who won't believe and who might trample and tear us. Others feel that it prohibits a Christian from being a judge over non-Christian people who, because they lack the Christian nature, might thoroughly tear and rend him. Still others think that Jesus is warning against surrendering the holy pearls of high ideals and morals to the "swine" of society in order to get them to think that you are a "jolly good fellow." Still others interpret it as meaning that the precious pearls of personality should not be abandoned to the dogs of drink and lust or to the hogs of greed and appetite.

It is an admittedly difficult passage, but since there are so many interpretations of it, perhaps one more won't hurt. It seems to me that this is Jesus' knockout blow against self-righteous, censorious judging. "The holy thing" means that which is set apart, sacred, or in this case, confidential. "Pearl" is a frequent figure for knowledge, particularly rare knowledge, or a secret. Now the verse reads, "Don't give that which is confidential to the dogs, neither let swine in on your secret." In other words, there might come a time when you come into possession of a big, juicy, confidential secret about someone. It's just to good to keep, so you whisper it "confidentially" to the next-door neighbor. He turns out to be a poodle who barks it all over the neighborhood. If your information happens to be false, of if it is successfully denied, the "dogs" and "swine" will put all the blame on you, walk contemptuously over you and tear you to pieces for being a liar and a gossip. And all the while your remorse will be adding fury to the fire.

So the kingdom citizen will neither tell evil nor repeat it to swine and dogs. If he is the bearer of unpleasant truth, he will either keep it to himself or tell it only to those who will use it constructively for the redemption of the erring one. It will be his desire to join with the Master in "healing the brokenhearted and setting at liberty them that are bruised."

# 12 Power Through Faith and Discipline

"Ask, and it shall be given you; seek, and ye shall find; knock, and it shall be opened unto you: for every one that asketh receiveth; and he that seeketh findeth; and to him that knocketh it shall be opened" (Matthew 7:7-8).

"Enter ye in by the narrow gate: for wide is the gate, and broad is the way, that leadeth to destruction, and many are they that enter in thereby. For narrow is the gate, and straitened the way, that leadeth unto life, and few are they that find it" (Matthew 7:13-14).

*Read Matthew 7:7-14.*

When one compares the strong, victorious, kingdom citizen whom Jesus described in the Sermon on the Mount with the weak, anemic, spiritless life of the average Christian today, one wonders what has happened. Did Christ aim too high? Was he too idealistic? Was his faith in the possibility of the kingdom of God on earth a fanciful dream? Or have men been too slow to believe? Has our lack of faith caused us to be earthbound and prevented us from mounting up with wings as eagles? Have we been unwilling to submit ourselves to the kingdom discipline and consequently failed to receive the kingdom power?

Clearly the fault lies with us. High aims and high ideals never handicap men. It certainly would not have helped us if Jesus had lowered the kingdom standards to the point where they would be within easy reach of the weakest person. If anything, this would have made us still more powerless. What we need is not lower goals, but the strength to obtain the goals which are set.

Jesus taught that this power for achievement comes principally through two channels: faith and discipline. There is nothing secret or mysterious or psychic about them. They are not offered as shortcuts to power and peace of mind in three or ten easy lessons. Yet they are big ideas, loaded with tremendous possibilities. It may be safely said that if one expects to achieve any measure of spiritual power, these two ideas will be the most important factors.

Speaking of faith, Jesus said, "Keep asking, and it shall be given to you; keep seeking, and you shall find; keep knocking, and it shall be opened to you. For every asker receives and every seeker finds and to every knocker it shall be opened." Does this mean that if you pray hard enough you can get anything you want? Is Jesus saying that God is a celestial Santa Claus who always brings good little boys and girls what they ask for? Surely not. It simply is not true that you can work up to such a stage of influence upon God that you can wangle anything in the world out of him. He isn't a Heavenly Vending Machine that is set in motion by a ten-cent prayer.

Jesus seemed to assume that God is already in motion, that he has already answered every prayer, that he has already prepared every possible blessing, already opened the door of his might, and also that God has already come to the very threshold of our heart with the answer to our every need. The problem was not to learn the secret words or the magic formula which would cause God to respond favorably to man's promptings, but to open up between man and God a mighty channel through which God's already prepared power could flow. On the human side, this called for faith. Man's faith, or lack of faith, was the determining factor.

It was a source of constant amazement to Jesus that men drank so sparingly from so great a reservoir. They were too timid around God. The Father had prepared so bountifully and sumptuously for his children, and they were too bashful to eat and drink. They starved themselves needlessly. They believed too little. Their faith was too small. If it had been only as large as a mustard seed, their faith could have generated enough power to move mountains. He wondered why men held God back so, why they were so unbelieving, why they hindered God from doing the many mighty works he stood ready to do.

When he did find faith among men, he was lavish with his praise of it; and when he found an absence of it, he was stern with his rebuke. When people asked to be healed, his frequent answer was, "Be it unto you according to your faith." His own magnificent faith was a tremendous thing. It appears brilliantly in the raising of Lazarus. When the news of the serious illness of his close friend reached him, there was no frantic excitement. With the calm, unhurried reassurance of one who knows that everything is well in hand, he went right on with his work for two more days and then announced that he was going to Lazarus' home. The disciples reminded him that due to the hostility of the Jews, this might cost him his life. He answered, "Are there not twelve hours of daylight? If one walks in the daylight, he doesn't bump into things, because the sun lets him see; but if anybody walks in the nighttime, he does bump into things, because within himself there is no light" (John 11:9-10). His argument was that there is as much daylight in the world as there is darkness, that the case for faith is certainly as good as the case for fear, and that though it might be a perilous thing to walk in the open daylight of faith, it isn't nearly so dangerous as sneaking around in the blackness of fear. Modern psychology certainly substantiates this, as well as the fact that if a man chooses to walk in the darkness of fear with no faith in God to light his way, *"within himself* there is no light." With his resources alone, man is incapable of dealing with his fears. He hasn't yet learned to use one eye as a flashlight while seeing with the other. His light must come from outside himself.

So Jesus chose to go to Bethany and risk being stoned rather than lead a life tortured by fear. It must have cut him deeply when one of the twelve, who no doubt regarded himself as a realist, whimpered: "Let's go, too, so we can die with him." Like many so-called "practical men," Thomas looked upon Jesus' faith as sheer folly. It wasn't good common sense. Yet Thomas himself was so afraid that he weakly resigned himself to what seemed to him a suicidal course. Jesus walked to Bethany in the daylight of faith; Thomas walked in the night of fear. Jesus went expecting life; Thomas went expecting death.

But greater than the faith that took Jesus to Bethany was that which he expressed in his prayer at the tomb of Lazarus, who had been dead four days. "Father, I thank you *that you heard me,* for I know that *you are always listening for me."* So strong was Jesus' faith that he assumed that *the event had already taken place,* that God had already answered. After thanking God for having heard him, he did not say, "Lazarus, arise," for faith said that Lazarus had already risen. What Jesus said was "Lazarus, come on out." And he came out, still bound with the grave clothes; then Jesus said, "Turn him loose and let him go." (See John 11:1-44.)

If this appears to you an impossible miracle, remember that nothing is impossible to the God who created the world and life in the first place. The Gospels are clear in their picture of Jesus as the supernatural Son of God. Remember also that even scientific research and experimentation is based upon the theory that he who asks receives, and he who seeks finds, and he who knocks has the door opened to him. If men didn't believe this, there would be no laboratories, no experiments. The whole scientific procedure is based on a confident assurance that truth already exists and that it can be found.

Of course, scientists know, as did Jesus, that although seekers always find, they do not necessarily find what they're looking for. Columbus wasn't seeking *for America* when he discovered it, but he was seeking, and doing so in the bold faith that he would find. Without such a faith, he would have lacked the power of persistence, which is one of the fundamental elements in finding or achieving.

But even though the seeker will not always find what he believes he will, Jesus assures him that what he does find will be equal to or go beyond his expectations. The father will never shortchange him, or make him accept shoddy goods. "For is there any man among you," Jesus asks, "whose son shall ask him for bread and he'll give him a rock? Or if he should ask for a fish, will he give him a snake? Well then, if you, weak mortals that you are, are capable of making good gifts to your children, don't you think your spiritual Father will give even better gifts to those who ask him?" (Matthew 7:9-11, *Cotton Patch Version*). He is saying that generally men *do* receive what they ask for. If a son asks for bread, the father usually responds with bread. But in those cases where he responds with something else, it is never less, but more. The heavenly Father *never* gives a stone or a snake to one who asks for and expects to receive bread or fish. If he makes any substitutions at all, they will be in keeping with his "how much more" nature. If men's lives are weak and devoid of the good things of the spirit, it is not because God cheats them. With their lack of faith they cheat themselves. The words of Jesus are eternally true, "Be it unto you according to your faith."

The greatest "substitution" — if one can call it that — which the Father makes is the gift of himself. This same passage in Luke reads: ". . . how much more will the spiritual Father give the Holy Spirit to all who ask him?" (Luke 11:13, *Cotton Patch Version*). The greatest gift anyone can give is the gift of self. "He that spared not his own Son, but delivered him up for us all, how shall he not also with him also freely give us all things?" (Romans 8:32).

In giving men the Holy Spirit, God also gives them the kingdom. When Jesus tells his disciples to "seek the kingdom," he adds: "Don't get scared, little flock, because your Father has decided to give the kingdom to you. Go ahead and sell your possessions and give evidence of mercy" (Luke 12:32-33). The Holy Spirit and the kingdom! These are the "good things" which the Father gives to those who ask him. When one receives them, he will never complain that his faith has not been sufficiently rewarded.

Since what the Father gives to us is as good as our expectation or better, Jesus said, "Therefore, everything that you want others to do for you, you yourselves do even so for them. For this is the law and the prophets" (Matthew 7:12). God doesn't hold back in his dealings with us. Just as any true father gives himself to his son, God gives himself to us. Then he treats us as well as or better than himself. In other words, God applies the "Golden Rule" to us and he naturally expects us to use it in our relations with others. *It is* fatherly love in action. It means that the kingdom citizen will treat his fellowman not as a brother but *as a son* to whom he has given himself. Truly this is the "law and the prophets," for in it lies the answer to all the problems of human relationships.

So then faith, which opens the door to fatherly love, is a mighty thing. But so is discipline. "Approach life through the gate of discipline," says the Master. "For the way that leads to emptiness is wide and easy, and a lot of folks are taking that approach. But the gate into the full life is hard, and the road is bumpy, and only a few take this route" (Matthew 7:13-14, *Cotton Patch Version*).

The truth of this statement is evident in every area of life, whether it be athletics or art, music or mechanics, science or storekeeping. If one wishes to "enter into life" in any of these areas, he must do so through the narrow gate. Through strict discipline he must confine himself largely to the thing in which he wishes to excel. To spread one's energies over many activities will weaken and finally destroy one's effectiveness and power.

Take dynamite, for instance. It is a powerful thing, but in order for its power to be released *it must be confined.* You can't get results by laying a stick of dynamite on top of or around the thing you wish to move. Gasoline is the same way. It generates power to turn the wheels of your automobile only when it is confined to the narrow walls of the engine's cylinders. A river, too, when it stays within its channel, is capable of generating electricity and bearing mighty burdens of commerce on its shoulders. But if it spreads out over too great an area, it becomes a swamp and is good only for breeding wiggle-tails and snakes.

Jesus felt that many people were making this mistake with their lives. In their efforts to be "broadminded" or "well-rounded," they were dabbling in everything and excelling in nothing. They followed every whim, fad, and fashion of the day. They changed jobs frequently, transferred from one college to another, moved from place to place. They never seemed able to wear the bridle of discipline so as to channel their energies for long upon any one thing. They were walking the wide, broad road to frustration and emptiness. Insanity would be the lot of some; unhappiness the lot of all.

But not all were taking this road. A few were hitting upon the narrow way. And it wasn't any rougher, or harder, or more unpleasant than the other way. It just wasn't as wide. At times it was sheer joy to travel it, for the flowers of accomplishment bloomed along the way. And the farther one went, the less tired he became, and the more infrequent were his periods of depression. Really, it wasn't a bad road — just narrow. If the roughness of the road was reflected in the faces of the people, it was much smoother than the broad way.

But Jesus wasn't explaining how to become a great athlete, or how to play a piano, or how to be an artist or a scientist, even though his principle holds true in these fields. He was addressing his disciples and telling them how to enter into life. There can be little doubt as to what he meant. He was saying that his way — the way of the kingdom — was in many respects a narrow way. It called on men to quit gallivanting all over the world and dissipating their energies in all kinds of schemes, cure-alls, clubs, societies, brotherhoods, orders, and organizations, and to get into the one channel of the kingdom fellowship. His way asked men to stop roaming the wastelands of their self-will and submit themselves joyfully to the group discipline of the kingdom. It made room for supreme loyalty to no other save Jesus Christ.

Narrow? Yes. Difficult? To be sure. But even though those who hit upon it are still few, it is the only gate which opens out upon the vast expanse of life. Every other way is a blind alley. Christ has made known "the way which he dedicated for us, a new and living way" (Hebrews 10:20). It's up to us to walk in it.

# 13 Clear Call to Christian Action

"Every one therefore that heareth these words of mine, and doeth them, shall be likened unto a wise man, who built his house upon the rock: and the rain descended, and floods came, and the winds blew, and beat upon that house; and it fell not: for it was founded upon the rock. And every one that heareth these words of mine, and doeth them not, shall be likened unto a foolish man, who built his house upon the sand: and the rain descended, and the floods came, and the winds blew, and smote upon that house; and it fell: and great was the fall thereof" (Matthew 7:24-27).

It is one thing to enter "the narrow way" of discipline and complete dedication to Christ and the kingdom; it is another thing to keep on climbing this upward trail. Sometimes people start this new way of life with great vigor and enthusiasm, soon become discouraged by the dangers and difficulties, and then sit down to wonder if they've chosen the right road. Jesus wanted men to understand that he wasn't taking them on a picnic. He was desperately anxious that they go with him, and yet he pointed out that there would be pitfalls along the way. He wanted them to count the cost and be prepared for difficulties. His warnings undoubtedly helped the disciples to succeed. One of the things to which they were to be alert was hypocrisy. "Keep your eyes open around pseudo-preachers," he warned, "who approach you in the guise of sheep but inside they are bloodthirsty wolves." The false prophets were dangerous because they were deceptive. Outwardly they looked like one of the sheep. They had respected titles. They had been graduated with big degrees from outstanding schools. They were in high places of responsibility. No doubt they had written numerous books which made them authorities in their chosen field. They were gifted speakers who could tailor their addresses to fit any audience.

But inside they were different. While they were careful to appear as kingdom citizens, their real motive, whether conscious or subconscious, was to devour the sheep, to sabotage the kingdom movement. Its way of love and humility and sharing was such a rebuke to their way of prejudice and exploitation and greed that they just couldn't stand it. And being smart, they knew that fifth-column, inside activity was more effective than a frontal assault. Their first work, of course, was to separate the sheep from the shepherd, for it was next to impossible to plunder the sheep when he was around. It is quite possible that the sheep were told not to be too loyal to this shepherd named Jesus. "Were not other shepherds around just as good as he?" they asked. Besides, they could not know for sure that he really was a shepherd; maybe he was just a creature of the imagination.

When these false prophets had thus destroyed the sheep's faith in their shepherd, it was an easy thing to kill their souls with such fangs as "the-time-isn't-ripe," or "don't-go-too-fast," or "it-would-be-good-if-everybody were-for-it," or "you'll-get-into-trouble." Then it wasn't long until the fake religionists had the kingdom message and witness diluted and cooled to a point where they were perfectly comfortable just to talk about it. The sheep were all dead or wounded, and the wolves were again the custodians of the status quo.

Jesus said you could recognize these gentlemen not by their bleats, for they had learned all the phrases and shibboleths, but by their fruits, their actions, and their living habits. "You'll be able to distinguish them by the way they live," he said. "You know, you don't gather grapes from a bramble bush nor peaches from a chinaberry, do you? So it is, a cultivated tree makes cultivated fruit, and a wild tree makes wild fruit. It is impossible for a cultivated tree to bear wild fruit, or for a wild tree to bear cultivated fruit. Any tree that does not produce cultivated fruit is chopped down and thrown into the fire. That's why I told you that you could know them by the way they *live*" (Matthew 7:16-20, *Cotton Patch Version*). Men and their institutions can be classified as Christian only insofar as they are true to the form of the original New Testament pattern. They must be measured on the basis of what they *are* and *do,* rather than what they say.

> *Lord, give us Thy Spirit now we pray;*
> *Reveal Thyself that we may see*
> *Thy cross! And rise up to follow Thee.*

And there must be action of more than just the lips, for the next thing Jesus warns against is lip service. "Not everyone who says to me, 'Master! Master!' shall enter the kingdom of heaven, but he who does the will of my Father who is spiritual." Entrance into the kingdom is not based on mere profession but on acceptance of a will and a way. A pious repetition of Jesus' name is no substitute for a life of loving obedience to the Father. A "worship service" is of little value unless it leads to worshipful service.

It's an old, old story — the pathetic, tragic sabotaging of the kingdom movement from within the sanctuary. The Christ of the fields and marketplaces has been entombed in cathedrals and holy places, and has been rendered innocuous by making him Lord of the lips and the hymnbooks. Frequently, art has been employed to remove him from this world. Thus, men who found that his life had made too great demands upon theirs got rid of him by exalting him to another world of existence, which left them free to continue their life here unmolested. With the skillful use of Scripture verses, they developed maps and plans for finding him only in the next world. There was nothing wrong with the way they said, "Lord, Lord." The error was that their way of life was so foreign to his.

There was still another kind of people that Jesus told the kingdom citizens to keep their eyes on. These people not only said, "Lord, Lord," but they had some mighty works to back up their profession. "The time will come when many people will gather around and say, 'L-o-ord, oh L-o-o-rd, *we* sure did preach in your name, didn't we? And in your name *we* sure did give the devil a run for his money, didn't we? *We* did all kinds of stunts in your name, didn't we?' Then I'll admit right in front of everybody that I've never known you. Get away from me, you wicked religious racketeers" (Matthew 7:22-23, *Cotton Patch Version*).

These people had the right words and the right works; the right creed and the right deeds; the right profession and the right expression. What was wrong with them?

120

Two things betrayed them. (1) They were too conscious of their good deeds. Their works were not a spontaneous expression of a loving heart, but a carefully planned program of a contriving heart. Obviously their motive was reward. Some might have wanted a starry crown and a long white robe from the Master so that they could receive through eternity the adulation of men and angels. Others would have settled for the delicious sense of superiority which they felt belonged to those who "serve the underprivileged." They were employees in the Father's house, serving him for the Saturday paycheck, rather than sons and daughters loving him for what he is. (2) While they called Christ Lord, they evidently thought of him as a means to an end. They made it clear that *they* did the prophesying, *they* cast out the devils, *they* did the mighty works. Of course, they used his name, but it was a mere tool, as though it were an ax in the hands of a person chopping down a tree. Instead of letting Christ use them in building his own kingdom, they used him in furthering their own humanistic, philanthropic schemes.

Here then is the sabotaging of the kingdom movement with "Christian service." Men set up their own substitute kingdom which they hope will bring them the rewards they desire, whether it be a life of tranquillity hereafter or a life of peace and plenty here. Then they map out their own schemes for either a "plan of salvation" or a "course of social action." Christ is called in to implement either or both. It's really a kingdom of man in which God figures, rather than a kingdom of God in which man figures. Quite naturally, Jesus could find little in common with the conceited citizens of the kingdom of man. They were subversive agents upon whom Christ's humble citizens might well keep a watchful eye. Paul, the aged, warned young Timothy to stay away from them, describing them as "having the looks of goodness but rejecting its power" (2 Timothy 3:5). He didn't want the Christian fellowship taken over by those who participate in the program of Christ but who do not partake of his Spirit.

Having warned against quack religious leaders, against worship without service, and against service without worship, Jesus draws his sermon to a close with a powerful exhortation to absolute obedience to him. He says, "That's why the man who hears these words of mine and acts on them shall be like a wise man who built his house on the rock. Down came the rain, up rose the floods, out lashed the winds. They all beset that house, but it did not fall. It was on *rock* foundation.

"And the man who hears these words of mine and fails to act on them shall be like an idiot who built his house on the sand. Down came the rain, up rose the floods, out lashed the winds. They all cut at that house, and it fell! And my, what a collapse!" (Matthew 7:24-27, *Cotton Patch Version*).

These words are so simple and their meaning so clear that comment is hardly necessary. Yet it is a profound parable. Jesus holds up two men who were alike in many ways. Both were hearers, perhaps sitting next to each other in the same pew. They read the same Scriptures and sang from the same hymnbook. Both were builders, each erecting his own dwelling place. And both faced the same torrential rain and flood and hurricane.

But there were differences. The man who heard and

did was a sensible man; the one who heard, and perhaps agreed, and did nothing more, was foolish. The first built on the rock; the second on the sand. The wise man weathered the storm; the fool went down.

With this parable Jesus placed upon his congregation the tremendous responsibility of classifying themselves. Their response to *these* words of his would determine whether they were wise men or idiots. He had given them the kingdom manifesto, had described the kingdom citizen, proclaimed the kingdom standards of righteousness, offered the kingdom of God *on earth* as a specific proposal for a new world order. Now he lays it squarely in their laps. Will they accept it or reject it? Will they hear it and praise it, or hear it and build it? In brief, will they wisely repent or foolishly continue in their same old order?

If they elect to act upon "these words," that is, to accept his kingdom proposition by becoming citizens, they will be given no guarantee against storms and floods and hurricanes. The same big problems and difficulties which beset persons in any social order or way of life will also beset them in the kingdom. Both individually and collectively, kingdom citizens will get their share, and perhaps more, of stormy weather. But they will be in a better position to ride it out, for they are founded upon the rock of a better way.

So Jesus not only calls for action but *the right kind of action*. The foolish fellow's trouble was not that he failed to act, for he, too, had a house to build. In fact, his excuse might have been that he was "too busy" acting upon a thousand and one other things. But he did nothing about *"these* words of mine." His failure was in doing the wrong thing, in building up the wrong foundation.

No matter how feverishly and ingeniously men fashion their systems, no matter how lovely their architecture, no matter how adorned with human blood and brains and sacrifice, unless it is "the city which hath the foundation" (Hebrews 11:10), "great will be the fall thereof." As Tennyson sang:

> Our little systems have their day;
> They have their day and cease to be;
> They are but broken lights of thee,
> And thou, O Lord, art more than they.

All around us we are hearing the crashing of our civilization, as one tornado after another rips it apart. Individuals, homes, communities, and nations are collapsing at an alarming rate. If the experiences of the last fifty years prove anything, they prove that modern man, in spite of his tremendous scientific achievement, hasn't found a decent way of life. He has learned to build houses, but he doesn't seem to understand the nature of foundations. He is skillful, but he isn't wise.

Jesus could be of infinite help to modern man if he could be made to realize it. The kingdom is no fad. It has been carefully tested in the laboratory of human experience and found to be as solid as God's eternal, spiritual laws. It is a safe foundation for any civilization. God wills that men should build upon it. There is no other way.

> The world planners gather.
> The young men mixed red blood with blue water
> And windy sands covered shattered helmets.

The old men confer with figures
And refashion their empires.
They seek a solution; they have it,
And they know it not.

Once when the world was younger
Some nineteen hundred years,
A quiet man walked the Judean hills
And along Galilee's shore;
Then men left their nets.
And he spoke to the people
On a mountain with loaves and fishes,
And he entered the city on a burro,
And they hailed him emperor —
And they nailed him to a cross.
"The Kingdom of God is among you."
They worshiped his teaching
But were afraid to live it.

The world planners gather,
They seek a solution; they have it,
And they know it not.*

When Jesus finished "these words" about the king·
dom, Matthew says that "the crowds were amazed at
his teaching, for he was teaching them as one who has
authority, and not like their scribes." That's a perfectly
normal reaction. No one can listen carefully to these
words without being amazed at Jesus' wisdom and depth
of thought. Yet the Master would rather have one devoted disciple than a multitude of amazed admirers. He
wants the loyalty of men, not merely their praises.

* Arvel Steece, "World Planners," *Christian Century*, March 20, 1946.

Which shall we give him? Shall we truly grant him authority over our lives? Shall we arise and forsake all and follow him? Our answer shall determine our future and that of the world.